WHY ON EARTH

?

A guide to success in your mission on this planet

LETICIA PARMER

BALBOA.PRESS

A DIVISION OF HAY HOUSE

Balboa Press books may be ordered through booksellers or by contacting:

Balboa Press
A Division of Hay House
1663 Liberty Drive
Bloomington, IN 47403
www.balboapress.co.uk
1 (877) 407-4847

Print information available on the last page.

ISBN: 978-1-9822-8111-3 (sc)
ISBN: 978-1-9822-8110-6 (e)

Library of Congress Control Number: 2019919367

Balboa Press rev. date: 11/27/2019

Acknowledgements

Thank you to all who have taught me so much. My cherished children for opening my mind to the magic of possibilities and my heart to love, and to my beloved mother and father for playing the roles I had requested they play on the stage of my life so that I might be provoked into following my passion and sharing my gifts.

Thank you to my magical and wise life partner, Quinto for his patience and inspiration, and to all who helped make this book happen, Maggie for support, Yinka for creative encouragement, Ali for enthusiasm and input, and most of all Angie, whose dedication, sharp eye and practical suggestions were of invaluable help.

Thank you also to all the multitude of people who have brought a lifetime of teachings, from my sacred clients and loyal students to the wonderful wisdom-keepers I have encountered along this life's extraordinary journey.

Prologue

Why are we on Earth
and how can we navigate this adventure
successfully and happily?

A mixture of psychology, astrology, ancient and original wisdom
to guide you through the journey of being human.

This book is a collection of vital knowledge, an abundance of which has been directly downloaded and given in visions and channellings, much has been gratefully received from the many wisdom-keepers I have had the honour of meeting along the way, and some gleaned from modern pioneers, but most of all I have learned from the long line of beautiful people I have had the honour of helping and working with as a lifelong Astrologer, therapist and healer.

I sincerely hope these insights will help you on the journey through your human life. My goal is that it will stir within you a deep soul resonance of remembering.

My innate sensitivity blesses me with the ability to vision and to connect with spirits, which in my lonely and challenging childhood was a great help and comfort. However, on reaching my late teens I tried to shut down my sensitive side. In an effort to fit in with what I saw was a tough and inhospitable world, I tried to toughen up, to close the channels that were constantly offering downloads to me. With little self-worth I set off on a wild thrill-seeking adventure, but at 21, I was brought up short, shocked into remembering my connections and shown how my extreme sensitivity and gifts did indeed have a purpose and a place.

From that life-changing moment I have shared my knowledge and connections in the quest to improve the lot of humankind, because I understood that the true purpose of my sad and lonely younger years had been to grow in empathy towards those who suffer and to to share my gifts in order to help make their human journey more smooth and hospitable.

Each client or patient triggers a deeper opening to compassion and understanding. I see and feel the pain in others and it has been my eternal mission to offer those who seek clarity and support during the tough times, the tools with which they can make sense of their journey, restore their own power and wellbeing, and remember who they truly are.

From my beginnings, born into a family with an atheist, scientific father and a raptly religious, judgemental mother, I was able to observe both extremes. In my bid to understand life and people's behaviour, I became fascinated by astrology as a tool to unravel the mysteries of the human spirit and to explore personality and purpose. Even to this day I never cease to find these maps of each individual life to be utterly fascinating.

Later, while living in America, I was called to the Shamanic path. Hungry for learning and connection and keen to add to my healing skills, I immersed myself in the traditions and practice of Shamanism, seeking out, and absorbing from, the knowledge of as many wisdom-keepers as I could find. Further studies with Mayan priests in Guatemala gave me a much greater comprehension of the universe and our relationship to it. Now I combine all my gifts and knowledge in my daily practice of healing individuals who have become lost or damaged in their struggles to find and stay on their true life mission.

The Mayan calendar shows that we entered a new 2,165 cycle in 2012. This Aquarian age leaves behind the human way of looking outside of ourselves for the answer but instead encourages us to go within to both develop and embrace our individuality and reclaim our personal power and authority.

I see evidence all around me that this is happening. In each person I observe a central pillar of Light that is growing through their human experience, personal exploration and spiritual development. It seems we who have incarnated now have chosen to be here through this momentous period of change. Through turning back to deep inner connection and trust in our individual selves, we each grow our own pillar of Light in order to become ready to offer our particular gifts outward, then unite with others to work together as an illuminated body of humanity.

So it is, that in order to feel truly connected and a part of the great body, we must ironically first truly embrace our singularity, our originality, our aloneness, our spiritual beauty and our perfection as a solo, one-off, yet perfectly designed, individual. Only then are we ready to share with the group.

I hope you enjoy the wisdoms and tips I share in this book as much as I have enjoyed the extraordinary journey that has brought them here.

Contents

CHAPTER 1
Beginning at the End

My first awareness of death came when I was two years old. A family pattern, as it turned out, because both of my parents lost family at that tender age. My mother's father was drowned on the torpedoed ship that should have brought him home on leave from war to her, a mere toddler. My father, aged two, endured the shock of losing his four year-old brother to a freak accident while playing. At their tender ages they were still in that phase of life where we believe we are the cause of all that happens in our world and therefore begins the conviction "It must be my fault, what did I do wrong, how can I undo it?"

The high sprung pram, all polished chrome and black, stood proudly in our hallway in readiness for my baby sister. My mother, usually tense, nail-biting and preoccupied, had calmed during this pregnancy and spent more time with me, which I relished. Aged only two, I delighted in the new, slower pace of my mother and in her attention. In our frenetic household with two lively and mischievous older brothers and a philosophical but somewhat distant father, my innately nervous mother was usually too distracted and tense to stop and give me much more than a sharp look or an anxious comment. Now it was different, her body insisted she take breaks, her condition made her calmer and kinder. As her belly grew she would gently place my little hands on it lovingly saying "this is your baby sister or brother, they'll be here soon, someone for you to love and play with. Here is the pram where we'll place the precious baby when it arrives, and where the infant will sweetly sleep."

Some weeks later, that object stood ominously in the hall, looming over me, casting a shadow in my heart and across my mind. It was no longer a symbol of new hope, it had become a thing of doom, a stark reminder that something terrible had happened to my mother, to me, to our entire family, because my baby sister would never be coming home.

In place of the magic, the dream my mother and I had woven together in those precious intimate moments, there was stark coldness, confusion and a massive sense of loss. There was no comfort to be had from my father either, as he masked his grief by focussing on my brothers who, sensing the change in atmosphere, ramped up their need for noise and disorder. As for my mother, she was 'absent'. Shock and unfounded guilt had sent her beyond grief into a complete breakdown. I lost her. She took to her bed to recover. I was dropped. The contrast from her loving tenderness to this complete unavailability left me in utter confusion and misery and eternally seeking the flaw in myself that surely must have caused this hurt, this shift in the family unit, this disaster, this emotional isolation.

I was not able to gain comfort from my mother. She was 'resting', then gradually returned to her household duties, but as an automaton, emotionally unavailable. She was back to being overwrought, never again to resume that gentle, intimate, loving space we had shared for those short months of her pregnancy. I lost her then, forever. Not physically but emotionally and mentally, and her shock, grief and self-blame were reflected in me. I ached for comfort and in the lack of reassurance, my internal longing and confusion were able to arrive at only one conclusion. It must somehow have been my fault that my little sister suffocated just as she was being born. Otherwise my mother would have surely come back to me with comfort and the love she had shown me before the tragedy which took away the sister who was to have become my playmate.

Fear grew inside my heart, that I was somehow basically flawed, wrong, bad, though I knew not how, so I was at a loss how to fix it. I strove forever to make amends, to be "good" enough to perhaps earn some love back from my distraught mother and to earn some time and attention from my confused and increasingly distant father. I was later to learn that the baby had simply been born with the cord around her neck, and despite the hospital staff's frantic efforts, she could not be saved. It was no one's fault, but after this tragedy all in the family shouldered the confusion and self-blame and reacted to it in their own particular way.

Two years old is a tender age to encounter the ripples and waves of loss, or to be plunged into a sea of grief, watching those we need to be a tower of strength and support, themselves crumble, themselves lost, themselves searching for help. To make sense of it as a mere two-year-old, to see my rock, my sustenance, dissolve in shock and mourning, unable to fix the problem, unable to comprehend its cause, nowhere to go with my grief and longing, I took the blame.

My mother's sudden coldness was a shock. I was innocent of the fact that she had tried to terminate this fourth pregnancy early on and was thus now engulfed in guilt, or that she'd grown to love and look forward to this new little one who had not been dissuaded from surviving the pregnancy, or that it was my mother's own colleagues, nurses like herself, who delivered her a perfect baby girl, blue and strangled. Had I been mature enough to know these things I would have understood that none of this, my sister's death, my mother's breakdown, my father's unavailability, had been of my making. But I didn't, and it branded me for life.

Somewhere inside of me, some infant logic told me I needed to be extra GOOD to earn and keep my place in the family. I longed for that mother I'd glimpsed, warm and tender, connected to me and sweet. Now, feeling neither nurtured nor reassured, I didn't realise that a seed had started to grow in me. A seed of fear. Fear of my mother. Something deep, dark and unmentionable. Unconsciously a terror crept in. If I hadn't killed the baby, maybe she had! Thus, as her moods became increasingly bitter and aggressive, I shrank back into the shadows. There was no safety here.

I was four when one afternoon the doorbell rang. I followed my mother and stood behind her skirts as she opened the door to a police officer. "Did you know the little girl?" I heard him say. He was talking about my four-year-old friend across the street, the girl with whom I'd been sharing playdates and at whose house I had been playing only yesterday. But today there was just the police officer saying "We are making enquiries, I am sorry to tell you we have taken the mother away, it seems she has killed her daughter". My mother's legs buckled and I felt the wave of shock and fear engulf me. Nowhere to run to, nowhere to hide! This was a subliminal confirmation. Mothers do kill their daughters. Another vow to myself, I would have to be EXTRA GOOD, just in case my own mother decided I was too much!

I was lonely and afraid. My mother's tension and stress, depression and aggression ruled our world. I adored my calm, kind and gentle father and longed for him to scoop me up and become my saviour, but he kept out of the firing line as much as possible, each day leaving as early as possible for work and arriving home long after I was asleep. Weekends he huddled away in the workshop he had made in our garage, taking my brothers with him, teaching them the magic of craftsmanship and engineering, but leaving me as 'caretaker' to the 'problem' mother. Oh how I longed to be included in their world of companionship and fun, in the fold of the menfolk, in their calm, creative, adventurous and fascinating kingdom, but instead I was relegated to the house where the 'dragon', the 'problem', dwelled.

My kingdom became our small back garden. A place of escape where I could find peace and connection. The trees, plants, insects and birds were kind, they did not judge or scold me, they soothed me, accepted me and all became my friends. More than that, they became teachers. It was quite normal for me to feel their moods, sense what they were needing, understand what they were communicating and to share mine back with them in an easy telepathy or speaking their language with them. As these effortless connections were formed I encountered such an abundance of love from all the beings of nature, such truth and reality, that outside felt more like home and family than inside the house. The natural world had become my true solace. Immersed in nature, I was at peace and never alone as I could connect with plants and with creatures of every size and type, learning their tongue and their ways, hearing their thoughts and their habits. We shared something I could not find elsewhere and it was abundant with love. Under the open sky with the smell of earth in my nostrils I would become lost in a space of peace and communion until my reverie would eventually be shattered by my mother's angry or irritated voice hauling me back into her agitated world of rules, imperfection, frustration and dissatisfaction.

I hated school. I couldn't focus, always afraid to make a mistake as I anticipated my mother's sharp voice pointing out a failure, a wrongness, making it clear I should be ashamed of myself and needed correcting. A lifetime of these anxious criticisms had left me with little confidence. I barely spoke except in a whisper, walked with my head down trying to stay invisible, too filled with fear to hear the teachers' words or respond adequately to their requests. School reports were always shaming "could do better", "should try harder". But I was in hiding, my world of imagination or time spent in nature, my only safety, my refuge of joy.

As I started to turn the corner into womanhood, with no reliable role-model and eternally seeking guidance, I experienced a life-changing moment. I was 13 when a girl in the playground brandishing a book demanded "When is your birthday?" On telling her May 1st she read carefully "You are plodding, thorough, stodgy, fixed, stubborn, unimaginative, immovable". I was indignant. "No, that's not me!" I quietly protested " I'm quite changeable, full of imagination and I'm always flowing with everyone else's wishes, where are you getting this from?" To which she replied "It must be true. It says so in this astrology book". In that moment something shifted in me. Little did I know this was the pivotal moment that would change my life forever. The flame had been lit, the path before me had opened up and I was about to find the guidance that had been lacking my whole life!

After school that day I went straight to the library and searched out books on astrology. I was determined to prove the girl in the playground wrong! She had described someone that was not me with such conviction that I had to get to the bottom of it. I decided I would simply show her why astrology was not only inaccurate, it had to be absolute rubbish.

What a surprise was in store for me when I opened those books. My first encounter with the ancient art of astrology revealed an intriguing door that beckoned me to step through, and on the other side of that door a whole world began to unfold before my eyes which was far deeper and far more complex than "I'm this sign, you're that sign". It was technical, detailed, meticulous, scientific, with fascinating diagrams and charts and a whole history going back to ancient times. The more these books revealed to me, the more I became amazed, hooked and intrigued. Little did I realise back then that I had started on an obsession that would last my whole life and become my life's work. Here were the keys I had been looking for, the keys to understanding human nature, human purpose, human beings. Perhaps also the keys to understanding my own family.

My rational mind had sought to confirm that planets couldn't possibly explain in detail who we are or the way we behave. Yet as I began to learn from those books how to draw up a natal chart, its accuracy astounded me. It was laborious work, maths was by no means my strongest subject, yet so enthralled was I that I was prepared to labour over logarithms to convert ordinary time into sidereal time (star time) and thence be rewarded with the makings of the map, onto which I'd place planets in their correct locations in the houses on this chart wheel and, *voila*, a complete picture emerged!

At first I drew up my own chart, over and over again, unwittingly I had begun intense training. The absolute magic when interpreting those planetary placings, was that it gave me an incredibly detailed and spot on description of my character, gifts and challenges. I became intrigued to look deeper, I needed to see if it worked with other charts, I had to explore further. So I began working on the chart maps of each of my family members, and time after time it was more than spot on, it was a window to their inner worlds and motivations, to their innate gifts and strategies, and personality types. I was able to understand at last what made everybody tick. I had found the key and I was hooked.

Eventually, having exhausted that source of individuals, I started drawing up and analysing friends' charts. Over and over the chart would describe the person's characteristics perfectly. There on the paper was the essence of their unique personality, their innate gifts, their natural career path, even the dynamic they would have with their own parents and their own children. All in such detail and without fail the information revealed would be absolutely accurate, right on target. I had the visual codes, the keys to the secrets of the soul, EVERYTHING! This was truly astounding!

I gave up trying to understand the 'how', I simply knew for certain, astrology worked and was a phenomenal tool for comprehending humans. Of course I had no idea at the time that part of my insatiable drive to comprehend people had been imprinted in me by the unconscious aching longing to crack the code of my unfathomable mother. I was unaware that with each chart I cracked, I was somehow getting closer to being able to read my mother, then maybe, just maybe, I could obtain an ounce of that love and understanding I ached for, from her. Nor was I aware that the drive to analyse and delve into the 'science' of astrology reflected the quiet analytical scientific way of my father and thus in some way brought me closer to him too. I was, however, aware that I possessed another sense which I could employ in my divination of any chart, a sense that was honed during my lonely childhood. The ability to hear messages and intuit knowledge, basically, to download information from guides and spirits.

By the time I was 20 friends were saying "You're really good at astrology, you should do it professionally". Surely not, I thought, that's not a proper job. Yet I had run out of people to draw up charts for, so I gingerly put my toe in the water and advertised my services as an Astrologer. A simple postcard in the newsagent's window "I will read your Astrological Chart" and my first client materialised. Oh, now it was 'game on'. It was all very well doing this as a hobby, but to actually charge a fee and take that step into the unknown with complete strangers, that was another matter entirely. Would it still work?

I was nervous as I met the lady, my first client, in a cafe. To make matters worse, she had a poker face, so I was not going to receive any feedback or acknowledgement during the reading. She sat still and silent as I commenced. My confidence could have been shaken, but with so many charts under my belt I had absolute faith that the information within her chart could not be wrong. So, as she stayed unresponsive, I took a deep breath and dived in. As soon as I started, I was back in the zone of certainty about astrology's gifts and my accomplished, somewhat psychic, way of interpreting a chart. I ploughed on as she remained still, listening but not responding, not even the twitch of an eyebrow! After one of the longest hours of my life, when I had explained in detail what her chart revealed, everything about her self, her family and her life, her gifts and challenges, I sat back and looked up at her. She simply shook her head in wonder, jaw dropped open saying "How can you know me THAT well, you've never even met me before?". Phew! It worked just as well for complete strangers as it always had for the people I knew. Yes, it still worked even when I was being paid to do a chart professionally. Thus my career was born.

Thousands of charts and all these years later, I have learned so much. One of the many gifts from astrology has been the knowledge that each of us is unique yet we are all PERFECT just as we are. I have never seen two charts exactly the same, even identical twins charts, of which I have done a few. The subtle differences, even when there are only minutes between birth times, are clearly shown. Each chart is composed of the same ingredients, just differently mixed. I have had the privilege of spying on humanity while being equipped to unconditionally reassure them of their perfection while showing them that they are on track. I have had the great honour to be the map reader for the souls who wanted a reminder of who they truly are and what they came to Earth for, in order to help them get back on their personal path to knowledge.

I love my work with a passion. It was not a plan but more of a natural evolution that astrology would become my career. So I am eternally grateful to that girl in the playground who unwittingly provided the spark that lit the flame of passion in my heart, and to the unseen guides and spirits who not only befriended me in my lonely childhood, but have stayed with me to help guide and interpret my readings, healings and the sharing of love and understanding for all the facets of my fellow humans. Also, through my quests for understanding I grew to realise who my mother truly was. Instead of trying to fix or change her, I accepted and felt compassion for her journey. Now I realise how blessed I have been that she brought me all those experiences and learnings that were tailor made, in order to motivate me into becoming the healer I am today.

THE GREATER GIFT

Little did I know that one year after that first astrology client, I would receive the greatest opening to wisdom I would ever experience. Knowledge shown and given to me directly from Source and so profound that it could never have been gleaned from the written word. I had to experience it, and from the moment I received this teaching my life was changed forever.

When I was 21 I died! It was not at all what I had expected to happen as I set off on my big travel adventure. All my life I had been enamoured with the idea of exploring new horizons, seeing fresh landscapes and experiencing different cultures. I had a huge curiosity about the world, about life, about people. I wanted to know more. Just after my 21st birthday my dream was to come true, I was about to satisfy that inner craving.

Between us, two friends and I had saved up enough money to buy an old VW van that was being retired from use as a school bus. We lovingly converted it back into a camper, with our quirky finishing touches of hanging swinging kitchen utensils at the back and painting a neat red cross on our first-aid box. We were ready to hit the road. The carefully made plan took us through Europe, first stop the Netherlands to visit friends, then all the way south, to end up in Greece. We joked that if we ran out of funds we'd probably end up treading grapes at a winery. It was to be the trip of a lifetime so, after a brief interview with the local newspaper who liked the idea of our adventure, we were off.

The first inkling that something strange and dangerous was about to happen occurred as we drove north through the Netherlands.

A certain disquiet descended upon all three of us. By the time we reached The Hague each of us had to admit to feeling a strong sense of foreboding. We didn't know why, but we all felt that something dreadful was waiting in the wings. What could it be? As we parked up in the back streets of The Hague we wondered if we were being warned of a potential break in. So we took all our valuables out of the van and up the long flights of stairs with us to the friends' attic apartment, where we were to be guests for a couple of nights.

The following night, disaster struck. Our hosts had sweetly put on a party for us and invited some friends and all the neighbours who lived in the building which, being student quarters, was divided into many little bedsits and flats. It was 3 am and just one or two guests lingered. We were dancing to loud music up in this attic apartment when I noticed a strange flickering orange light outside the window. Our host, together with my dance partner, raced off down the stairs to investigate. I followed. Down the steep wooden stairs, along a landing, down another flight, along a landing and down more stairs, only to encounter the front door shockingly ablaze! Worse still, the flames were already high and starting to lick their way up the staircase towards us. The two boys turned on their heels and ran, stopping on the first floor landing to call out "There's a fire, close all the doors and windows!" to the inhabitants of the building. Then they retreated into the office on that first floor, to call the fire brigade. But I didn't stop running up those stairs I wanted to put as much distance between me and those terrifying flames as possible.

Desperately out of breath and in shock, on reaching the attic I saw my friend obliviously still dancing in the arms of the remaining guest. I tried to shout "There's a fire!", but as if in a nightmare my voice came out in a breathless whisper. Again I tried "There's a fire!" then turning towards the tiny kitchen my shocked brain started looking for a big pan to fill with water in order to douse the flames. Suddenly there was a tap on my shoulder. My friend said "Is there really a fire?", then seeing the ghostly shock on my face, she authoritatively said "Don't panic, come with me!". I felt gelatinous as she grabbed my hand and tugged me, off down the stairs. But after only a few steps we encountered thick black smoke. Separated now, we ran on into the smoke until it became a dense wall of treacle. I somehow reached the bottom of that flight of stairs desperate to take a breath, but none would come. I couldn't inhale, my lungs had shut down, they simply wouldn't inflate and my mouth was gaping like a fish out of water. Then the realisation hit me, there was NO WAY OUT! I was trapped. I could not possibly, with no breath, attempt to climb back up the staircase from which I'd come, and hearing the roar and crackle of flames below me meant that to go forward must mean certain death. I was out of options. My head went strangely calm and a stillness came over me. This is it then, I didn't know it would be like this, but this must be how I die.

Yet, like an automaton, my body continued to move forward along the pitch-black landing. My hands feeling my way along the bannister, I shuffled towards the next flight of stairs. But as my foot reached its downward step, that was the end. I was gone, a lifeless rag doll tumbling down those stairs.

To my astonishment I was suddenly no longer there at all, but travelling down a tunnel towards a bright light, which seemed to be beckoning me. As I was pulled inexorably towards The Light, there to one side was my beloved Nanna, smiling at me and nodding. She was a brief, comforting sight as on I went till I reached The Light, and standing before this incandescent illumination I was immersed in something I can never forget and cannot adequately describe in words. The Light before me emanated TOTAL, UNCONDITIONAL LOVE. A love beyond anything that could possibly be imagined here on Earth. A billion times more than the unquestioning love of a baby for its mother, a billion times more than the nonjudgemental devotion of a pet for its owner, this love was totally and completely all encompassing. It enveloped me, suffused me, overwhelmed me, awed me.

Time ceased to be linear in that moment. I was able to see everything about my life that had gone before, all my actions and experiences. Everything was up for review, and I JUDGED MYSELF. I felt regrets about things I had done and disappointments about things I had failed to do. In the presence of such enormous love I felt "I've let

You down", but to my utter amazement only love came back to me from The Light. There was no judgement of me whatsoever, except BY me. So, in response to my shame and regret, what came back from The Light, was total, unconditional love. I was bathed in it, enveloped in it, completely suffused by such eternal, limitless love that I knew everything about me was accepted and cherished, and in that moment I realised I had returned to the Source, I was back in the arms of love from whence I had originally come.

Next, I found myself transported to a garden, absolutely exquisite in every way. There was no density in the atmosphere. The colours were vibrant, every leaf and every petal was crisp in outline and in that moment, from the depths of my soul, I knew that I was *home*. A sense of relief suffused me, no more struggles, no more troubles, no more worries, I was at peace.

Then I became aware of smaller versions of The Light, and I saw that each was appointed to a human soul waiting to incarnate. As I watched I realised that each of these human souls was choosing the details of their next incarnation and beside each one stood a small being of Light, simply standing by as their appointed soul designed the details of its forthcoming life; choosing the gifts they would take with them to share with humanity, the challenges, difficulties and lessons they would encounter, even selecting the major players on the stage of their life to come. I observed each human soul make contracts with the souls who would play these roles for them. It was fascinating to watch this network of agreements taking place, these beautiful golden threads being woven into a tapestry of accord between souls who were offering to play specific roles for each other – parent, sibling, partner, child, teacher and so on, in their next lifetime.

As each human soul designed its own next incarnation, the being of Light beside them never interfered, never advised, never interrupted, just lovingly and patiently observed, unless that soul tried to take on more than they were capable of dealing with. Only in that instance would the being of Light gently offer "Maybe that's a bit more than you could manage". Other than that, the next incarnation with all its challenges and gifts was entirely designed by the human soul that would live it. When all was decided and designed, appropriate to the level of that soul, then the soul was ready to incarnate to live their life moment by moment, letting the mystery unfold, forgetting they had chosen every aspect of it beforehand.

Then I found myself before The Light again and I was being asked one simple question "What have you learned?" The response welled up from deep inside my being, and I felt disappointed to realise that I could not stay as I responded to The Light "I have not finished what I set myself to learn, oh no, must I go back and complete it?" The gentle, benevolent loving sense from The Light was "You know what you must do".

Suddenly I was catapulted back to the living world. I felt my body being jolted up out of the stairwell by human hands that had grabbed me and were pushing me into a smoke free room, the office on the first floor. I stood gasping in the doorway of that office, where the boys had found refuge. Hearing us crashing down the stairs they had opened the door and seen our bodies crumpled on the floor, then dragged my friend then me into this safe haven. Covered in soot and gasping for air, I stood in awe and wonder that I was alive and safe. But the roar of flames below us and the crackling pop of windows bursting from the heat, drove me to the only possible escape route – a big sash cord window. My friend's dance partner, who must have followed us down the stairs, came crashing in the door behind us. Desperately gasping for breath he raced straight over to that window and smashed it open with his bare wrists. I raced over as did my friend and one by one we jumped, then fell, then ran up the street in terror, away from that raging inferno. Shaking with shock, sitting on a dustbin, the whole street was lit up by the house, now becoming engulfed in flames. I looked on as the fire brigade arrived and started to rescue folks from upstairs windows, swinging them out over the street and onto their long ladder. I was alive, yet utterly stunned and awed by the soul learning I had just received.

I kept it to myself, that extraordinary, awe inspiring experience of going to The Light and what had been shown to me on the other side. I hugged that profound knowledge to myself, the strange and wonderful revelation of the truth of death and life. I told no one, believing they would think that I, or at least my story, was crazy.

Slowly, however, things started to come across my radar. My eyes would pick out a headline in a magazine or a title of a book, about near death experiences. It began to dawn on me, this was what had happened to me. Each story was something like mine, not exactly the same, but so similar that I started to realise that others too had visited The Light. But why me? Just ordinary me. Why was I permitted to see something most of us do not get to see till the day we die? Then I realised that, rather than shamefully hiding the details of my near death experience, I had been given an enormous gift, and sharing it had a true purpose.

It soon became clear what that purpose was. Though I was only a year into my career as an Astrologer, after the fire more and more people were 'by chance' finding me who were either dying, had a fear of death or had recently lost somebody. I had somehow become a magnet for those who had to know. I possessed knowledge they badly needed to hear. As they kept on coming, it was my joy to be able to share with them the beauty and the truth of where we come from, why we are here, and that our natural and timely death is nothing to fear.

I was able to share the knowledge that Earth is a University for the Soul and, as there are billions waiting for a place, how lucky we are to be here on Earth right now. Most importantly of all, I was able to remind each person I encountered of how supremely powerful they are because they chose their own challenges and inter-actors right from the start. I was also able to show them that their astrology chart was merely a map of what they had pre-chosen to be and to do. This helped them to release any sense of victimhood or blame and thus let go of judgement, either of themselves or of others. I was able to explain what I had been shown and understood. That our toughest times are the greatest gifts and that when problems arise in life we are truly getting on with our own set coursework, as it is then that we are on the fast track to soul learning.

From that fateful day of the fire, I was a changed person. I came away from the experience with profound knowledge and an extraordinary boost to my natural gift of intuition. The ability to receive divine insight and guidance direct from Source grew stronger. I could simply 'know' things and 'see' things that would be helpful in my life and to my clients. I could tune in to their soul state as much as their human state and if necessary I was even able to scan to see within the body for diagnosis and guidance on physical healing for the person before me. I was always given the 'key' to the source of their problem, and thus the 'key' to their healing. What a joy to be able to share these gifts with those in fear and in need.

Every day I have felt enormously grateful for these profound gifts, as my soul purpose is to help and heal those who are afraid, broken or who have simply lost their way. I know now that this is why I chose my own sufferings, and that is why I thank my parents most profoundly for playing the roles I had, on a soul level, requested them to play to facilitate such specific learning.

CHAPTER 2
You Chose This

The profundity of that near-death experience when I was 21, was to unfold month by month, year by year afterwards, and still teaches me to this day. Though I had always been a natural empath, able to communicate with animals, plants, trees and spirits in my solitary childhood, something shifted after my encounter with The Light. The ability to download knowledge direct from Source came easier and faster. It had always been there in a mild way, making me a bit different as a child; that inner knowing, those premonitions, those connections. But after the near death encounter, those abilities were truly magnified. It was as if an information channel had been opened. Over the years that gift has proven to be the generator of much healing and inspiration, helping me to deal with my own life lessons and assisting me in showing others the way. I am so grateful to my spirit helpers for supporting and advising so generously and reliably along the way. The downloads which came through at times of greatest need were an inspiration and a life saver, and as time went on they became more powerful for each client needing insights and help. I am always awed by how divinely I am given the key for each person, to turn the lock in their soul and release the truth of their healing, their balance, beauty, power and purpose. I am deeply honoured to be able to access these insights and to be in a position to heal through using them.

From that terrifying yet, ultimately, deeply enlightening experience when I was 21, I was able to realise and to absorb that my wounds and tragedies and those of everyone around me were not by chance. They were not dumped on any of us by either bad luck or a wrathful God, nor were they happenstance. I finally 'got it', that **we were never powerless victims**, but that each one of us, with our own free will, had orchestrated every tough experience that was to happen in our lives, and had done this for the divine purpose of learning. We had chosen with loving guidance on hand, our coursework for this **university for the soul called Earth** and had selected both our teachings and our teachers. In other words, WE were in the driver's seat and our free will was bringing us all the life experiences we needed to encounter. An utterly empowering concept which deletes any sense of helplessness, any fearful search for a saviour or victimised longing for rescue. Instead, it puts us firmly behind the wheel of our own journey.

I was able to release from my belief system that I had been a victim of a dysfunctional and critical mother during my lonely childhood, but to embrace, instead, the knowledge that I had chosen every experience in my childhood and that my mother had been a wonderful catalyst, bringing to me the exact teachings I had wanted and needed, and which, pre-birth, I had asked her to bring, as a part of my golden-threaded network of agreements between souls. In knowing this I released blame, judgement and victimhood, replacing it instead with compassion, understanding and the return to my personal power. I had been driven to astrology and psychology in an unconscious bid to understand and 'solve the riddle of' my mother, in the hope of gaining the love I craved from her. Now, it became clear that I had needed that motivation, to chase those and other teachings, more in order to fulfil my destiny, which was to share my knowledge to help and heal other lost souls.

As the years passed, my work as an Astrologer proved to be the most phenomenal training ground as it continuously awakened to and elaborated my understanding of the human psyche. I had the privilege, through analysing thousands upon thousands of charts, to look deeply into the situations and interactions, the struggles and the learnings, the gifts and the expressions of the human soul. As I observed each client's story, I was able to learn ever more about the human race's challenges, our desires, our destinies and our strengths. Seeing their path and choices so clearly and accurately mapped out, I began to notice patterns in my clients' charts. I could observe that people with similar planetary designs in their charts would encounter similar problems at similar stages in their lives, and would react in similar ways. This gave me a rich schooling in interpreting each aspect of the astrological chart map, and I began to realise that those who came to me for their birth map reading were in truth seeking a reminder and clarification of the original choices they had made before incarnating. As a therapist, seeing and knowing so many different kinds of human suffering, traumas and challenges in so many different ways opened my mind to comprehension and my heart to compassionate non-judgement.

So much was becoming apparent as I worked with humanity's designs and lives. One of the revelations was that the older the soul (the more times it had returned to the Earth University), the tougher the coursework that soul was able to take on. I understood that, as with grades in school, each time we incarnate our soul is able to take on a more complex and more mature level. Simply put, a Grade 8 level soul couldn't possibly cope with Grade 12 level work. This was why the appointed being of Light had not interfered with the soon to be incarnated soul's choices, unless the coursework that soul was planning to take on, was clearly more than they were capable of dealing with.

Thus, rather than pity those with the toughest lives, or see them as victims, they are to be honoured as much older souls than those for whom life seems to go more easily. For certain, the people who encounter the hardest tragedies are the oldest souls and therefore have been able to take on the toughest assignments. Knowing this truth I like to offer to you this advice. *When disaster or difficulty strikes, open your arms wide, throw your head back and say "Bring it on, I chose this for a purpose and I will grow wiser and my Light brighter through navigating my way through it, I am strong enough, I CAN do it".*

Prior to incarnation you were like a Hollywood movie director, setting up your life story and all those who would play roles in it. You chose all the life challenges that would facilitate your learning, and made soul agreements with those who would play the 'bad guy' in your life. But how you handle these challenges and what you learn from them are your day to day choices. That is why, in this book, I am going to give you many tips on how to make the journey smoother and the learning faster.

If we approach our troubles from an empowered, rather than a helpless, standpoint, we can step back from our woes and observe the thread of treasure running through them, and that treasure is the adapting, learning and growing we are being prompted into. Never imposed, this will always be a learning which we chose for ourselves long ago.

I was in my 30s and a mother of three children when my husband's job took us unexpectedly for a short stay in the United States. I was happy to go on this 2-year adventure, but after many months, I was starting to get homesick and anticipating the return to my country and extended family in England. Then that short stay was unexpectedly extended indefinitely! What was I to do? Feeling far from my homeland, my brothers and my ageing parents, I put a prayer in to my spirit guides "Why have you placed me in this location? Please show me, and help me to know the purpose of my being here". The answer came quickly and not at all as I had expected, which is so often the way of Spirit. A teacher appeared in my life, a wonderful wise Shaman who started training me in that ancient knowledge. This immediately resonated deep within my soul. Now, instead of feeling homesick, it was as if I had finally come home to the place I had always belonged, to my true self.

As a child my grandmother, a wonderful seamstress, had offered to make me a costume. Would I like to dress up as a queen, a ballerina, or perhaps a fairy? No, I knew exactly what I wanted. I longed for my fringed suede dress and moccasins. Because from very young I had recurring vivid memories of living in and missing my tribe. I know now that I was indeed hankering after the life I had previously lived as a Native American, that had been tragically cut short, at which moment I had made a vow to return to Earth and help when I could be of most use.

I was now in America and blessed to have found the wonderful wise Shamanic teacher who re-awakened deeply buried knowledge within me. From that beginning I was hungry for more. So I searched out other wisdom keepers who so kindly and gracefully shared their ways, their customs and their profound knowledge. Everything they taught me resonated so strongly, I knew it was more a case of remembering than hearing something new. No longer homesick to return to England, I was healing a much deeper and longer homesickness, to return to my original people. I joyfully incorporated this wisdom and these beautiful ways of respect, honouring the spirit in all things and staying open and connected, into my healing work.

I am eternally grateful to the spirits and to the many incarnated wisdom keepers whose own inspirations pushed me further along my forgotten path and confirmed inner knowings that had seemed so out of place in my modern life. Most especially my Native American brothers and sisters, both in the flesh and in spirit, who have given and continue to share so very much wisdom. By that first teacher and the many that followed, I was brought back to my connections and reminded of the profundity of humility and simplicity, and of the love available to us all from Great Spirit, nature and the cosmos. The ancient ways felt so familiar. It was a knowing that I already possessed, hidden deep within. I was being blessed, reminded of and shown the pathway back, to my soul's roots.

Thirteen years passed before I eventually returned to England. It was then that I heard a very loud prompting from my guides "Now you must teach what you know". I resisted, spent many days waking in a cold sweat and filled with self doubt, telling myself "How can you presume to know more than the next person? You can't sit in front of a group and behave so arrogantly" or "What if you are judged as coming up short" or "You might wear or say the wrong thing", until one morning the penny dropped. I awoke suddenly realising that all these self sabotaging warnings were truly my ego! **The ego which steps between the soul and it's self expression**, the ego of shyness and self consciousness. To teach, I finally recognised, was not about ME, I was simply to be a vessel and allow the divine teachings to flow through me to whoever needed to hear them. I clearly remember the down to earth message from my guides "Get out of your own way and get on with it!". It is wonderful how direct and often humorous messages from Spirit can be! Thus I started my first Shamanic gatherings and began to run courses to pass on the profound knowledge I had been so privileged to learn.

Through the wisdom and ancient teachings I received from so many wise ones, I was reconnected to what is real and what is valuable. I was reminded of the truth that we are all one, all part of and not separate from the loving spirits that surround us. These benevolent beings are within everything, the plants, the trees, the rocks, the animals, the insects and the birds, the waters and the skies of this planet. Each has a caring, generous and loving spirit presence, willing to help us if we simply ask with an open heart and a trusting mind. Learning to connect again with all these wonderful beings provided me with the support I needed to continue with my work. Reminding those who had lost their way how to embrace trust, conquer fear, reclaim innate power and open again their hearts and minds to love.

RELEASING JUDGEMENT AND BLAME

Our Earth walk is very precious. Of the billions of souls waiting to come to this University for the soul, we are the lucky ones who got a place. Make the most of it! Once you decide to re-incarnate, once you get to the front of the queue and gain a place, you start the process of setting your own course work. Entirely with your free will, you plan your course subjects or degree work, choosing all the aspects of the life you are about to embark on. Most importantly, the difficulties you must endure that will pummel and shape, carve and refine your personal block of clay into a beautiful sculpture, by stimulating those parts of your soul which have not yet blossomed. Simultaneously you also choose the players on the stage of your life, those who will help you in your quest to develop parts of your being, those who, through challenging you, rocking your world and taking you out of your comfort zone, or by enlightening and supporting you, will offer the perfect opportunities to make that growth you have desired happen. So, as you set up and cast the characters, be aware that you also set up the 'villains' because in fact it is they who will bring the biggest opportunity for your learning and growth. As you request a soul to step into a role for you, that soul comes forward and offers to play the part you need them to play. And in the perfection of synchronicity, they also need YOU to play the role of yourSELF in THEIR life. Each of you will be a catalyst for the other's learning and growth, thus this symbiotic deal is agreed.

It is fascinating to see the golden threads of these contracts between souls as agreements are woven into an incredible tapestry of co-operation. Some of us will play the good guy in others' lives, some will play the bad guy. It is interesting to consider, since each of us comes from divine love, it must surely be much harder to agree to play the 'bad guy'. Even more interesting to contemplate that those who do so in your life have made that sacrifice to facilitate your learning. It is strange, therefore, to realise we must honour rather than condemn, those who challenge us. After all they have taken on a difficult and unpopular role just for our personal growth, to help us in fact!.

Many religions preach forgiveness, yet, if you think about it, in order to forgive you must first make a judgement. That the person you will, so graciously, be forgiving has done you 'wrong' and is in some way 'bad'. We may mouth the words, we may believe we've righteously forgiven someone for their transgressions, but because we sit in judgement of I'm RIGHT and they are WRONG, forgiveness simply cannot close the chapter. Indeed, it is the very act of sitting in judgement over the 'wrongdoer' that binds us to and keeps us from ever releasing them from our energy field.

Every hardship has a deep and true purpose, often we cannot see this until after the lesson is done. Yet each adversity, each challenge, each suffering is a powerful instrument for growth and therefore, the person who has played the 'bad guy' has in fact helped you by providing the catalyst. Their challenge has triggered you to draw deeply on your own resources and character, not only to surmount the current problem but also to enhance an inner reservoir of strength that you can draw on in the future. Think of the many stories of humans conquering adversity in impossible situations. Those who have beaten the odds, overcome seemingly insurmountable difficulties and somehow made it through, have done so by drawing on their own deep inner reservoir. Where did that come from? How was it built?

Looking at a toddler learning to walk, they encounter many hurdles and need courage to keep on trying, despite the pain, they push on through knocks and disappointments until finally and triumphantly they have mastered the technique, which will carry them majestically through the rest of their lives. So it is with all of us, through adversity and the courage to keep going we gain just the tools we need to go forward and achieve our ultimate goals.

On the stage of life, we are each playing a role our soul chose before incarnation, which miraculously fits in perfectly with the individual soul growth needs of all the other significant people in our lives. If you were being cast in the movie of another's life, wouldn't you prefer to play the saint, the hero rather than the 'bad guy' or villain? Of course you would because, as with all humans, deep inside you are driven by love. So in fact those who offer to play the villain in our lives are making a huge sacrifice for our ultimate benefit. They will 'push our buttons' to be the catalyst for our comprehension and enhancement. So to put the final twist on it, they are indeed our greatest helpers. Holding onto resentment by blaming them we can never release them. Holding onto judgement about another's 'wrongness' puts us on a superior level, so there can be no chance for closure. Alternatively if you are able to see the gift of their performance in your life, recognising it simply as that, you remember you are mere equals on life's stage and in that moment you can reclaim your power, let them go and move on.

So it is with the world stage. There are those who have stepped up to the plate to play the role of villain, to facilitate the growth of the human race from complacency and the habit of sitting on the sidelines 'tutting', into a race which takes the right action for their fellow human beings and for the planet as a whole. It seems we take one step further along that path each time we THANK rather than judge our adversary.

In the microcosm of our most intimate life through to the macrocosm of the world stage, there will be those who pummel our block of clay into shape by challenging us. And you know, the challenges you have sustained in your life have been uncomfortable, painful, even shocking at times but ultimately they have grown you into becoming so much more than you were.

WHY ON EARTH?

So why on Earth am I here? What is MY PURPOSE.

How often I have heard this question from someone coming for healing or therapy, "What is my purpose?". There are many questions hidden in this one request. The answer to practical matters such as "What job should I be doing" and thus "What should I be studying" are easy answers as they can be clearly defined from my client's Astrological chart. Also the next level of meaning is "What gifts did I come to share with humanity?", that contract your soul made pre-incarnation, is also easy for me to clarify from your Astrological chart, but let us go deeper still. Why am I actually here on Earth?

Of course, having an opportunity to experience living on Planet Earth is a magnificent thing, there is so much beauty and wonder that we can enjoy and be inspired by here. However, why should we set ourselves hurdles and challenges? Why the tough stuff, what's the point?

The answer is that through each suffering we grow in compassion. We have BEEN there. So instead of simply imagining how that must feel in another human being, we KNOW, in our very soul, in our very cells. Because we have personally lived that tough experience our heart flies open. Each time we overcome adversity, we grow in comprehension and empathy for our fellow man, eventually into a state of non judgement. This comes from releasing the desire to over-rule, condemn or blame, and this release can only come from going through the very same thing they are now struggling with.

Only through adversity can our compassion grow and grow until we are wise enough to fully embrace unconditionality.

At the end of all these many lifetimes of soul learning what is the subject that we are graduating in? It is my understanding that in our growth process of many lifetimes, our goal is to arrive at the point of illumination where we have dissolved all barriers to total, unconditional love. Thus each soul must, in one lifetime or another, experience EVERY possible human condition. One lifetime the loser, another lifetime causing the loss, one lifetime the abused but in another causing the abuse, one lifetime betrayed yet in another lifetime the betrayer.

It can be a hard concept to grapple with, that anyone would CHOOSE some horrendous form of suffering. But in accepting this we honour the power and journey of each individual on the planet, respecting the fact that how their life unfolds is exactly as they planned it. They are not victims, they are supremely powerful.

Some years ago when I lived in America I met a beautiful soul, a woman who had herself been through a near death experience similar to my own and had travelled to The Light. She too had been shown the same teaching that we each plan our suffering and put in place the players on the stage of our lives, before birth, making those soul choices in order to facilitate our own and others' learning. Tragically she had lost her son, who had been murdered. She told me that each month she made the long journey to the prison to visit his killer and each time brought the same open hearted message "There is nothing to forgive. In my heart I understand that you and my son made a soul contract that this would be your journeys in this lifetime. I do not blame you, but instead I must thank you for playing the role you agreed to play for him". She KNEW without any doubt that all of them, her son, his killer and herself, had made a soul contract before incarnation that this was how their lives would unfold and these were the specific roles each would play. So, from her learning when on the 'other side', she gained such knowledge and profound wisdom that it awoke in her unconditional love instead of judgement.

UNCONDITIONAL is a kind of love that can only be learned through personal suffering which grows our inner Light of true empathy ever brighter. The tough stuff moulds us and softens us around the edges. We learn that the other beings on this planet are our equals, each on their own specific journey of learning and growth with their own set of troubles, burdens and tragedies, along with their joyful experiences. Each one of them is simply doing their best, as are you.

So it is that lifetime by lifetime we are building our personal experiences, playing the roles we must, until we have lived it all, until we truly KNOW first hand every possible condition and facet of being human. Only then can we cease to judge, but simply LOVE and only then can we join the angelic ranks to become Beings of Light ourselves.

Yet we are hampered and slowed by the debris from the past. In the forthcoming chapters I will share with you some powerful tools for moving that debris away, so you can travel forward more smoothly, with less trauma and more clarity.

CHAPTER 3
The Ultimate Learning Tool

You have already selected your mission and the major performers for your life journey, those who will play the important roles to facilitate your learning. You have chosen what you are going to learn, what experiences you need to go through in this lifetime for your Soul's growth and what gifts you will share with humanity. Now, with the design for your forthcoming lifetime complete, you are ready to incarnate and will live each moment as an experience with no recollection of having chosen it all beforehand. You are on your way!

You have come from the exquisite place of love, Light and harmony and you are ready to step into a brand new life, to start the next grade. The new term is on the brink of beginning, and this is when you collect your greatest learning tool - FEAR.

It happens approximately three months before birth. You become conscious that you are within your mother's womb, stuck in your own small human body which you are helpless and powerless to either sustain or maintain. Your soul is compelled to go forward, to become human, to complete a mission, yet you realise you are alone and have no control over this vehicle you are encased in. So you feel weak and helpless. This infant body that you now dwell in must survive at all costs. It is vital, therefore, for you to be taken care of when you arrive on Earth. But who did you choose to do this for you?

This is the moment when you receive the greatest tool of your learning, as your physical helplessness brings up the feeling FEAR.

You must survive yet you are not in physical control. You are in the hands of others whom you must trust to ensure your survival. You are utterly dependent upon these caretakers to look after your precious self. It is the mother and the father you have pre-selected who must be the essential sustainers of your physical vehicle, so they are absolutely **key** to your survival. You need to check them out. So you take an etheric look outside of the womb, at whom you chose to be your father. Is he strong enough to support and guide you? Fear rises in you as you notice that he has so much stuff going on that might distract him from being your pillar of strength. He may be worried about money, he may be anxious about whether he will be able to cope with another baby to be responsible for, he may feel trapped or even feel like running away. He may be frightened that he's going to lose his freedom or the devotion of his wife because now she is going to be focussing her love on this new arrival. He may not feel that he is able to be the unwavering, reliable support that your helpless self is going to need; your rock, your protector, your benefactor. He may even be a figure separated from your mother. Seeing his flaws so clearly, and needing to make him strong enough to be the support you vitally need, you take on some of his burdens to lighten his load. So it is in this moment that you energetically lift a bunch of his baggage and place it onto your own right shoulder.

Next, you take an etheric look at the one who must physically sustain you, with milk, nurturing, care and comfort, your mother. Boy, has she got a lot of issues! She may be nervous, tired, insecure, overwhelmed. She has so much going on, yet you are utterly dependent on her to take care of your physical needs, to keep you warm, to carry you carefully and most vital of all, to sustain you with milk! So you feel you must lift a large load of her issues from her and place them onto your left shoulder.

This lifting of some of your parents' burdens is not altruistic, you are not motivated by caring for them, your motives are entirely self serving, it's about THEM caring for YOU. Your motives are driven by the desperate need to survive. Now that you are conscious and feeling so physically helpless, you have to ensure that those people who are destined to be your vital support, will be emotionally strong enough. Your parents, who are going to be the caretakers of this infant body and keep the vehicle that is to carry your soul alive, must be capable of doing the job. So you have to lift off some of their burdens to help yourSELF. Having done this your infant consciousness says "Maybe, just maybe, now that I have unburdened them by taking on some of their issues, I might be safe, I might survive, I might get to complete my mission." Deep within you is a sense that there is quite a rocky road ahead, and your instinct to survive rules everything.

This is where it begins, this is where you start to carry fear, the ultimate tool of learning. Fear that you may not make it, that you may not survive, that you could fail on your invaluable mission and the bottom line....FEAR THAT YOU MIGHT NOT GET YOUR MILK and then DIE.

If it has been your choosing to be rejected by your biological parents and adopted by new ones, the key is about where your milk will come from. In your pre-birth quest for reassurance that you would be supported and taken care of, if you recognised that your birth parents would not be the ones tasked with this, you would have moved on to 'fix' your adoptive parents' issues and lighten *their* loads. Even heavier would be the burden of being partially bonded to your birth mother, then moved on to another who would take on the responsibility of bringing you your milk. The fear, in such cases, of being abandoned and unsupported, and the risk of not getting your milk is even greater. A profound and deeply embedded insecurity that you have chosen to learn from and grow past in this lifetime.

Carrying the tool called fear, and now programmed to save your parents at all costs to ensure your very survival, you are born. Birth in itself is an utterly terrifying experience. A moment of being squeezed and pushed and pummelled and squashed until, bursting into the atmosphere you must expand your unused lungs and draw your first breath. The breath that tells you whether you are welcome or unwelcome here, in Earth's and your family's atmosphere.

The tool FEAR that you've picked up travels with you throughout your life. It is how you will learn all the lessons that you have come to learn. Only through experiencing fear can we propel ourselves into the ultimate learning of our very souls. Throughout your life, as with your birth, the hands of destiny will pummel and squeeze, mould and shape your block of clay until, when you have finally completed your coursework, you will become the beautiful and shining sculpture of loving compassion and wisdom that was your original goal. So the battle of your whole life is on, the battle between your innate love-governed self and your adapted fear-governed self.

Although you made the design choices for your life, and although fear is the tool through which you will be challenged to learn what you came to learn, with this book you can master how to make this journey one in which you are empowered and wise enough to use the fear tool to best effect. And though you made those essential choices before you were born, each day of your life you still have the opportunity to make choices about your direction and actions, in order to develop yourself into a higher, brighter being.

RESCUING YOUR PARENTS

It is from that pre-birth moment of recognising your helplessness and dependence that you start a lifelong instinctual drive to save your parents. A need to fix them in order to survive. This basic programming goes underground, we have no awareness that it is driving much that is dysfunctional in our lives, colouring both our reactions to and our relationships with others and the world around us.

Unable to shake off the sense that we cannot manage without them, we watch our parents or caretakers from the start, sensing their moods, tuning in to their weaknesses, then do our best to bolster them up, keep them strong. Unconsciously afraid that we might lose this vital support, we adapt ourselves and our behaviour to make sure they remain intact. If we have been moved on from one set of parents to another, as in the case of adoption or fostering, then we experience a huge sense of failure and a far greater drive to keep this next lot strong enough to not also abandon us.

However, the drive to save our parents does not stop once we reach adulthood, it continues even after our parents have left the Earth plane. The actions we take and the limitations we impose on ourselves are regularly influenced by our need, ironically, to keep them strong enough to care for us. By fearfully holding onto the initial terror that without them we cannot survive, we have programmed ourselves, at all costs, not to destroy these essential caretakers.

This can cause us to limit ourselves, for fear of undermining or squashing our parent or caretaker, to protect them from their own emotional damage, even if it means damaging ourselves. When we are young we do this in obvious ways, trying to please, trying to be good and not make a fuss or being helpful to ease their burdens. As we grow into adults the parent rescuing goes undercover. We have no idea how much it unconsciously drives our behaviour and our reactions. This manifests in so many ways including copying their behaviour, even dysfunctional behaviour, to make them 'right', to justify them. For example, boring people with our terrible jokes, drinking to excess because they did this, chastising others with judgements as they used to do.

Often we will take on a partner who carries similar wounds to those of our parent so we can try to fix those deep wounds once again, but this time in our partner, the surrogate. Or, if our parent has been abusive or abandoning, we will choose to repeat the abuse by selecting someone who will do the same, simply to find our way through the maze of understanding, then overcome this flaw in them. Often we will do this just to make that parent 'right', because if they are right, if they are understood, if they can be made 'OK' then we can be safe, we will not destroy them, then our milk is assured and we will survive. This line of understanding is full of twists and curves, but if you can unravel it, then you will feel a calm serenity in your life as you truly comprehend your inner needs and motives to overcome the driving force of fear.

I had a client who was hugely talented yet every time he had an opportunity to gain success, to fly high in his career, something always went wrong. He was frustrated and disappointed and came to me for help asking why everything was set against him. He even wondered if someone had put some kind of 'curse' on him. He had lost touch with his own power and was now living in fear. He had no idea, that he was unconsciously self sabotaging, limiting his own chances so that he would not climb higher than his own father had managed to do, as this would energetically destroy his father.

On another occasion a lady came to me exhausted and upset because her career was demanding too much of her, leaving her little time or energy to spend with her children. It turned out that she had grown up hearing her own mother bitterly disappointed and suffering from depression because she had given up a career she had loved and which had defined her status. She had heard her mother constantly complaining that she had 'been somebody' before she married and had children, but now she was 'just a housewife and mother'. Unconsciously, therefore, my client had picked up and lived that wish for her mother, always driving herself as a career woman, relentlessly pushing herself to live the dream on behalf of her mother, and thus save her. Once she was shown this, the relief was enormous. She did not need to save her mother, she simply had to follow her own dreams. In fact, all she really wanted to do was enjoy time with her children and be a home maker, so she changed her life to happily follow her own heart, overcoming the fear driven programming that if she failed to save her mother, she would die.

Prompted by the fear of not surviving we start to run patterns to make our parent 'OK'. It is such an unconscious programming that we do not realise we are ignoring our inner voice of desire, our own dreams, until we lose touch with them and wonder why we feel dissatisfied. As adults we have no idea we are still reacting to our original pre-birth, helpless terror of our parents not being strong enough to be there for us. This anxiety can be distilled down to that same one overriding and most basic fear of all, in fact the fear that drives all our fears. **I might not get my milk, so I will die.**

IF I DON'T GET MY MILK, I'M GOING TO DIE

All babies cry when they're hungry. The infant, with hunger pangs and increasingly desperate that their next sustainment, their next milk, might not arrive, will cry out in fear and pain. 'I need feeding and

34

maybe this time no one will come, this time I might be abandoned, be left all alone to fade away'. The utterly dependent infant screams to have its needs met, terrified that they will die. As that little human grows to be an adult this primal drive is so imprinted that it does not leave, it simply goes into hiding, sliding beneath the surface of our awareness, but still very much active. We adapt ourselves, yet it is amazing to realise that always at the heart of all our fearful behaviour is that one goal, to get our milk so that we won't die.

Of course each one of us is at heart a being of love, that is our true essence, at our core. But the human fear of not getting your milk now overrides this. Fear, that great learning tool, is the opposite of love and the ULTIMATE FEAR, the fear that drives every human soul away from their own innate loving nature, that drives us into dysfunctional behaviour, is the fear of failing on our Earth mission, the fear of DYING. It is such a powerful key to understanding yourself and others, that all human emotions boil down to this.

Peeled back to the core of our feelings, it is simple. We can only come from love or fear. Those two opposing forces cause all the anxiety, confusion and stress in every human life. All human actions that are not driven by love – greed, abuse, rage, selfishness, cruelty, and so on - have fear at their core. All around you, in all negative human behaviour, you can detect this if you look deeply enough. If you peel back the layers of the onion to it's core, what will you find there? The feeling of helplessness that cries out "I might not get my milk, and if I don't, then I'm going to die".

Imagine you are travelling on the motorway and someone forces you to swerve because they are driving so dangerously, in a tearing hurry to get somewhere. This person may be a business executive on her way to the important meeting which will decide whether she is 'in' or 'out' of the deal. Her ultimate fear is that she will fail, be rejected from the group, cast aside, all alone, and therefore will not get her milk and will die. Or the driver might be a teenager desperate to impress his friends, because if he doesn't he might be out of the pack, left all alone, a reject who will not get his milk and then die. In fact, ironically the fear of no milk and thus the fear of dying can make people so desperate that they will behave in a way that might even kill them! Deep down we are all reacting to that programming and we act it out in many different ways, on a daily basis.

So I invite you to take a step back and observe human behaviour. This can be more than amusing, it is hugely valuable in gaining perspective and understanding rather than reacting to others negatively or with judgement. When you observe another person's seemingly unloving behaviour, detach yourself mentally, then strip back the layers of the onion of that human. Once you get to the core you will realise what is driving their negativity. Persevere, layer by layer and you will inevitably reach the realisation that they are actually afraid that they won't get their milk! Now, instead of becoming the infant yourself, responding to their fearful behaviour with fears of your own, you can stay calm and mature, remembering that you are perfectly safe, as you are actually big enough and strong enough to get your OWN milk, something they seem to have forgotten. Seeing people and situations in this way brings into your awareness and into your heart the ultimate healer and enlightener, humour. With this viewpoint your own fear is replaced with amusement and your condemnation will thus be replaced with compassion.

There are many ways in which we act out our primal fear. Are you a rescuer, believing you must save mummy or daddy in order to get your milk? Are you a people pleaser striving to be good, to ensure you can get your milk? Are you an attention seeker believing that if mummy doesn't see you, you won't get any milk and therefore you will fade away? Are you a complainer bawling your head off to make sure they know you exist, otherwise you will be overlooked and the milk won't come? Are you the one who has to be the shining star, to make your parents feel they have done a good job, thus saving them and becoming a hero just to earn your milk? Are you aggressive or competitive, fighting for your share of the milk, fearing someone or something could come between you and your sustenance leaving you to starve? Or are you self abusive, asking for nothing, for fear that asking too much from the source of your milk will cause them to not have enough strength to sustain you? All of these and many more dysfunctional adaptations in human behaviour are driven by that same basic need. Of course, at times we can be each of the above and probably you can see yourself in all of them. Yet each of these behaviours is driven by forgetting your state of love, which is where your true power is held.

THE FEAR MOMENTS

Fear versus love. Those two opposing forces cause all the inner turmoil, confusion and stress in our lives. From the beginning, when you first picked up that tool, fear, it has driven all of your negative reactions. You toddle, learning to walk, you fall, bang your head, scream in terror that this essential learning will never go right, that it will be too painful, and yet you start again, and again, no matter how many times you fall, until you have mastered that skill. Conquering fear to embrace our independence, our grace and our power is a major part of the human condition. We step forward into the unknown, we feel fear and feel driven ever onward to master our fears, to achieve our goals and beyond that, to re-inhabit our innate essence of love.

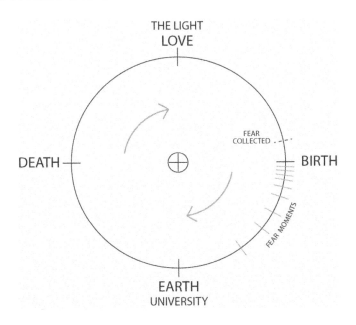

As you grow from infancy there will be many, many traumatic moments and each time you hit one of these, like a beautiful jewel, a little piece of you may fragment off. Moments such as the trauma of being born or the fear before your milk arrived. Perhaps falling and hurting yourself when learning to walk or more dramatically, the terror you experienced if you were truly abandoned or abused as a child. Each time, because we are too young, too inexperienced, too immature to deal with the shockwave of our trauma, the fragment of our jewel that breaks off becomes stuck like a freeze frame in a movie, too stunned to rejoin the jewel, which goes on developing without that piece.

Each one of these traumatised, and thus left behind, fragments is a wounded child piece that is now isolate and alone, but deeply in need of support and healing. They remain there, lost in the past, in that moment of powerless terror that shocked them and split them off. Later in life that piece will come up and haunt us with a reminder of that particular insecurity and fear, catching us unawares, especially in vulnerable moments. Those wounds sit deep in our human psyche and may ironically drive us to repeat them in some other form when we are older, until we have finally dealt with them.

One such example, a client in his 40s, had no idea that his periods of depression were being triggered by a horrendous experience when he was 12 years old. He had arrived home unexpectedly to find his mother, whom he'd always believed was his project to save from a violent father, making love with a stranger in his living room. He fled out, his whole world and the fabric of his identity, disintegrated. All the beliefs about whom he was and whom his mother and father were, the structure which he had built for the entire 12 years of his life, had come crashing down. He had always thought his role was to be the saviour of his victim mother and that to support her he must shun his father who must be the villain. Yet in this shocking moment he is confronted with the fact that the opposite is true, and if that is so, who was he now and where did he fit in. In that shocking moment he lost his identity and safety, he felt utterly alone. Heartbroken and with no tools to cope, he buried the experience as a large chunk of his own jewel broke away.

Later, in moments when life threw a curve ball at him, that wounded part would surface to say "You can't trust anyone and you have no true identity" and the depression would start. In relationships, he unconsciously kept choosing women who would betray him. Why? Because he needed to re-experience the feeling, so he could understand, make sense of and somehow deal with this horrendous wound. He had no idea that part of his driving force became a need to copy his mother's behaviour in order to save her by making her 'OK'. To justify her, and somehow make her 'right'. Still governed by the original fear that his mother would not be strong enough to sustain him, and thus he would die, he started to embody her negative behaviour. On a deep level he believed that by lifting and emulating her pattern he could make her behaviour ok and save her, thus he also became a betrayer.

The fragment of his jewel which broke off in that moment of shock, would sit on the sidelines, forever driving a cycle of disappointment, disempowerment and depression until, through therapy, he was able to perceive and re-integrate it. When he was able to meet, embrace and reassure that innocent and perfect part of himself, the little 12 year old boy so devastated, he was able to take care of him, support and heal him, ultimately integrating this lost part of himself and most importantly reclaiming his own adult confidence and power.

Each of your traumatic moments is etched onto your soul, into your deep unconscious. Later, each past fear has become a trigger which brings about an unwanted reactions in the present. Unless dealt with, this can go on right through to old age, often running a repeating, outdated, story from the past that starts a knee jerk yet totally unnecessary or inappropriate response and behaviour. The original, pre-birth fear of being helpless and unsupported was triggered each time you experienced a trauma in childhood. It has then acted as an unconscious reminder of your vulnerability, to once again magnify the fear, causing you to anticipate with dread the next thing that might happen. You expect a repeat, even though life and circumstances are completely different, in fact YOU are completely different. Yet the wounds and fears have created the mesh of your beliefs which to this day filter everything in your reality. The helpless child can haunt you and sabotage your maturity, your confidence and your power. The child that fears losing support, losing their essential parents and therefore needs to keep those parents safe or rescue them, is not equipped to do so. Yes, the adult is, but cannot do so without the right tools. In this book I would like to give you those tools.

HOW TO OVERCOME FEAR DRIVEN BEHAVIOUR

The forces that appear to restrict us actually provide a stimulus that motivates into greater personal achievement, enhancing our attitudes and abilities. However, we have been looking **away** from the box containing our fears, instead of **into** it. Opening it and disempowering our fears is the way to master them. Which means looking backwards is the only way of achieving smooth forward momentum!

Only by healing our childhood wounds can we re-integrate our earthly self with our divine original, pre-incarnation self. Then we remember who we truly are; innately powerful and perfect beings who are the essence of love. Unfortunately, in being too busy looking forward we dismiss the voice that calls us back, yet that's exactly where we need to go to collect the KEYs, they await us there, in the past, in our childhood.

Lifting the lid off that box of powerlessness and terror is how we reconnect with our true self, our strength and the inner spark of unconditionally loving consciousness that is our ultimate destination. You are not a victim and do not need rescuing because YOU are supremely powerful and perfectly capable of getting your own milk. Nor do you need to rescue the adults around you as they, too, can get their own milk.

LIFE CYCLES

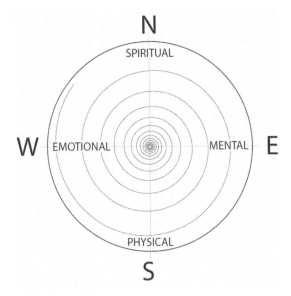

I am often asked by a client "Why is this happening to me again, I thought I had dealt with it?". I explain to them that we are all travelling in cycles and a great way to see this by looking at the meanings within the Medicine Wheel. In my tradition, the East represents the dawn, springtime and our mental state, the South represents midday, summertime and our physical state, the West represents sunset, fall time and our emotional state, and the North represents night, wintertime and our spiritual state.

By tracking our way around this medicine wheel it is easy to see how a newborn starts with mental curiosity (East, mental), then, moving on around the medicine wheel, they begin to feel a physical pang of hunger (South, physical), next they move on to feel the bliss and reassurance of sucking milk (West, emotional) and finally they arrive at oblivion, sleep and dreams (North, spiritual).

In the above diagram I show how that spiral is small at the beginning of our life then grows bigger. A new baby comes from The Light (the centre of the medicine wheel) and every hour moves through each of the four energies, to do a complete circle on the Medicine

Wheel. At the beginning this takes a mere hour, then this expands to every two hours, then every four hours as their journey spiral gets wider and takes longer and longer. Eventually, as adults, we still hit these metaphorical points on the wheel as we travel along our life path of learning, but each time it will be different depending on our acquired life skills and how much experience and learning we carry with us to help us master that same challenge when it reappears in a different guise.

CHAPTER 4
Relating To Other Humans

In this Chapter, I will give you keys and insights into how to improve all the relationships in your life, whether family, personal or business. As you begin to see beneath what is initially obvious to you about how all humans interact, you will be better able to relate to them and to develop a profound understanding of yourself too. Remember, **you are perfect just as you are in your deepest self.** However, that true self may have been buried by layers of adaptation, guilt, self sabotage, resentment and fear. In the previous Chapter, I advised you that to attempt to forgive others doesn't work. What I will add to that is, **do** forgive yourself.

THE PERSON WHO WON'T CHANGE

The image of a snake shedding its skin came to my mind when I started to write this chapter. In Shamanic tradition, snake represents the ability to shed the old skin in order to allow for personal growth. The metaphor is clear. When we are ready for growth, we must leave behind the ways of being that we have simply outgrown and stretch ourselves into the new more awakened persona. When we are ready, we slough off the skin that no longer fits and inhabit the new skin of the self we have matured into. Yet we resist this uncomfortable transition and all too often get into trying to change another person rather than go through the inevitable transitions that must happen in ourselves. This may be quite unconscious, but in seeing their mistakes and flaws, we can't help but go about the business of trying to fix them.

Imagine for a moment that you encounter a snake and YOU decide that it is time for it to shed a skin instead of allowing this event to happen naturally at the perfect moment for that particular snake. What a time wasting and risky task you'd be taking on. You could try every strategy in the book but It would be impossible to loosen its skin and force the snake to slough off. For each individual snake this can only happen naturally, when the time and place are exactly right. Such interference will make the snake do everything in its power to escape or, if you persist, it may turn on you and bite you. Likewise, if you try to force change on a human being you will probably become frustrated and hurt.

So it is in relationships. None of us can decide when it is the right moment for another to shed their skin or grow into a new one. Each human, as with each snake, must listen for his own inner prompting that growth is ready to happen, then the shedding of the old skin is a personal, very gradual process. Each soul must feel from within their spurs and promptings to personal change. To assume you can do this for another is arrogant, insulting and ultimately futile as it will cause both of you pain.

Instead, take personal responsibility. Remember, you are the only one who is running YOUR life and you have neither the right nor the power to force change on another. To do so is presumptuous and a judgement, that they are not making the right life lesson choices for themselves, that they are not an empowered soul running their own unique coursework and that their time frame must be dictated by you.

One of the reasons we focus our attention on fixing others is the unconscious pre-birth programming we picked up, to fix our parents. The person you are trying to fix may be a substitute for the actual parent, but the driving force inside you to fix them is the same. Another, more elusive reason for focusing all your energy and attention on trying to get someone else to shed a skin, is that it keeps you too busy to do the real work you came here for, that of looking within and sloughing off your own outgrown skin.

THE IRRITATING PERSON

When someone irritates us, pushes our buttons, our first reaction may be to complain about them to another. Remember, whenever you point the finger out, there are always three fingers pointing back at you. In other words, your criticism of another is always really about an aspect of yourself that you are not comfortable with, which has just been reflected back at you. At such times it is good to quietly ask yourself "What is it about mySELF that I do not like in them?" You'll be surprised and enlightened if you are willing to go there, even more so if you are willing to accept the uncomfortable truth in the answer you get. It is not our first reaction to do this as it is far easier to point and blame. But if you can embrace the concept that the reaction has come from you so of course it IS about YOU and thus this person has actually provided a mirror for you see an aspect of yourSELF that you dislike, it will create a wonderfully fertile soil for your own growth and more harmony in your dealings with others. Taking personal responsibility for our own feelings and motivations is paramount in finding inner happiness and therefore happiness in all relationships.

In Miguel Ruiz's inspiring book The Four Agreements, he recommends, *'Never make Assumptions'* and *'Don't take anything Personally'*. It is amazing how quickly we leap to conclusions when in dialogue, or when observing another's behaviour. It is a powerful exercise to look at what conclusion you have reached, then trace back in your mind step by step, how you got there. You will see that you have raced from A straight to Z, riding on the wave of your own wounds and assumptions without truly, dispassionately seeing the facts of the person or situation in front of you. When ruled by our wounds we may assume all sorts of things that simply aren't the case.

When it comes to taking things personally, check yourself to see if you personalised a neutral comment when it really wasn't aimed at you at all. Taking things as a personal attack will alienate you from the one you are with and if you carry on down either of these tracks you will grow further and further from reality, thus distancing yourself from harmonious co-operation and resolution. In future, if someone irritates you, see this as a gift that will enable you to take a mental step back in order to see some aspects of yourself you refuse to love.

HOW WE INSTINCTIVELY RELATE

How each of us relates to others is deeply flavoured by the earliest influences of our time on Earth. The first relationships we have with our parents and siblings, extended family or caretakers and teachers, form dynamics that will colour all relationships in our future. The first five to six years of our existence on Earth are hugely influential on how we will react to and cope with our experiences and how we will dance with the personalities we encounter.

We arrive on Earth, we find our place, we learn compromises and by the age of six we have developed a personal identity, a core personality. It is how we slot into the world we find ourself in. I have named it the 'I'M THE ONE THAT...' identity. For example, *I'm the one that has all the responsibility on my shoulders* or *I'm the one that isn't visible* or *I'm the one that is overruled and disempowered.* Long past the age of six, we continue to react to life from that original standpoint, not realising we have created a kind of prison for ourselves. We believe that 'self' is our true identity and, though it may be in some ways dysfunctional, we cling onto it, as without it we wouldn't know who we were. The truth is you can break free from any pattern or box you have placed yourself in because **you are the power** in your own life and can make of it anything you wish. The knowledge and the tools in this chapter will help you do this.

The entire human race has evolved through adaptation and so it is that we adapt to fit in and find our place from the moment we are born. In nature, energy takes the path of least resistance, like a twig in a river, in order to keep flowing forward. When you first arrived into your family you found your place within it. Like a child arriving in a classroom where every other seat was taken, you headed for the only available seat. From the very start of your life, therefore, you intuitively recognised where your place must be, you read the situation and slotted in. Thus the adaptation began.

We are going back in time, here, to take a look at how you may have been influenced and your character formed in those earliest years, by how you had to adapt from the very beginning. So, when you arrived into your own family, which was the only seat left available for you to take? If the family you were born into was full of dynamic, attention grabbers, you may have taken the only available place left, that of the quiet, invisible one. If the family you were born into was full of anger, you might take the place of the passive one or the peacemaker. If the family you were born into was full of rescuers, you could easily have become a victim. So the place you take in the family dynamic, the only seat available, hugely influences your forming personality and all future relationships. Let's take a deeper look at this placing we have in our family group, and its enormous influence on our forming personality.

The oldest child, or only child, takes on the anxiety of new parents who haven't trodden this path before, and often feel the need to push through their fear in order to prove to the world they can do it. Also, in this case, the enormous weight of their parents' responsibility of having to make sure everything is safe. The oldest child feels the parents' nervousness so decides they must take charge of things as there might be no one capable of doing so. Then if siblings arrive, the oldest child experiences loss and grief as all the love and attention poured onto them is now diverted and diluted. Indignation and the need to 'fight for' what they want can set in. **Persecutor** mentality can develop here as this soul, seeing itself as the one who must carry the burden for their parents and now for their sibling as well, on whose shoulders all the responsibility falls, becomes assertive and bossy to keep things on track, to keep things safe, and to 'save' their parents.

The middle child feels they had a status as the baby of the family until it was taken away. Then they just become the filling in the sandwich, un-noticed, unseen, lost, valueless and invisible. The one above them has a set status, the oldest and the one below them has taken over their own original status of adored baby. Insecurity can either keep them super amenable and bending to everyone else's whim with sweetness and light in order to be loved, or their desperation to gain attention can turn them into the family clown and mischief maker, just to be seen. It is easy for the middle child to become a **rescuer** as they develop the belief that only by being a hero can they become visible, can they earn some love, can they have a value.

The youngest child feels restricted and overpowered, even bullied. They are expected to be the eternal baby doll of the family as everyone above them needs to treat them as helpless and imposes their will. Their own desires overridden, they start to resent the more capable souls who continue to dictate or tie their shoelaces for them long after they can do it for themselves. Independence and respect denied them, extreme frustration or apathy can set in with a feeling of 'What's the point in bothering', as all their self motivation is stifled. As an adult, this person can become quite the **victim**, acting disempowered as they apathetically wait on the sidelines for someone else to pick up the pieces for them, or play needy as it is their learned method of gaining some attention, yet at the same time they feel resentment towards those who reinforce their sense of powerlessness. They also learn to manipulate as it is not safe to be direct about their goals.

TAKING THE STANCE OF VICTIM

You have come to this University called Earth in order to learn and you have set your own coursework. It's not always easy, it can be quite daunting and as you travel your path some struggles may seem overwhelming. Yet you plough on through and eventually 'earn your diploma' as you come out into the light of illumination and mature wisdom. Some folks go to actual university with the full intention of succeeding at their chosen studies but then find the challenges and coursework so daunting that they become paralysed with fear. Convinced that they can't cope, they find a place to hide, maybe the university bar, or by getting someone else to do their assignments for them or feeling everything is futile and that they are innately a failure, and giving up altogether. This is a metaphor for life, and describes those people who give up on their 'coursework'. Unable to take on the life challenges or soul moulding struggles they set themselves, they hide away in alcohol, drugs, affairs, gambling or other escapist manoevers that keep them from making any progress on a soul level, leading them to stagnate, give in to their fears then feel ashamed and lost in a self destructive cycle.

This spiral keeps going downward, and ironically it is much harder to climb up out of, than it would have been to have faced the life assignments and emotional challenges they were trying to avoid in the first place. Using the metaphor of the university, seeking out a wise counsellor when those fears first raised their ugly heads, might have avoided the paralysis and self sabotage that crept in and wasted precious opportunities to learn and mature.

Another way to hide from your own life assignments is to play the victim then draw in others to 'rescue' you, to handle the tough assignments for you. Wouldn't it be easy if they just gave you all the answers, perhaps even wrote the thesis for you? Then they could alleviate the slog and struggle of doing it yourself, they could fix it so you had no challenges to overcome, no work to do at all. Yet of course that would defeat the whole purpose of your incarnation, because YOUR SOLE PURPOSE IS SOUL LEARNING. By handing off the work you would never learn a thing about your chosen subject and exhaust the rescuer who already has their own full programme of coursework to do.

When the victim ensnares the rescuer a dysfunctional and unhelpful dance begins and there are no winners. The victim is wasting precious learning time, not facing their own challenges head on and growing weaker in character every day. Simultaneously they are sucking energy from the one they have bribed, guilt-tripped, persuaded, emotionally blackmailed or bullied into doing the hard slog for them to get them off the hook.

Ultimately, it simply doesn't work because all the victim is doing is putting off the moment when they will HAVE TO learn that particular thing, either in this lifetime or the next. The lessons we have set ourselves will not simply disappear no matter how many rescuers we line up, nor how many avoidance tactics we try. Instead they will simply wait in the wings until we are ready to face those challenges head on. That is why I encourage you, when suffering, troubles and life challenges come along, to open your heart and mind by making it clear to the universe that you are up for the challenge, you recognise it will be tough but that you will gain enormously by going through it. Remember my advice from Chapter 2. Open your arms wide and shout at the universe *"Bring it on, I came here for this and I am ready to learn what it is I have chosen to learn, because I know it will make me stronger"*.

We take on so many challenges when we choose to come back and be human again, from the first moment struggling to be born and taking our first breath, to mastering the skills of walking and talking, from the painful growing of teeth, to the physical or social challenges of growing older. Yet each challenge brings us immeasurable rewards and empowerment, once we've mastered it. No one can do it for you and yes, it can be daunting or painful, but through courage and perseverance your soul's rewards will be immeasurable.

A good exercise to remind yourself of your own power is to look back to a prior challenge you overcame, and notice who you were before the difficulty and who you became after you mastered it. Be proud in remembering your courage, your achievement and your strength and that will help you to remember that no one else can do it for you, and that you do have what it takes to grow through this latest challenge, ultimately gaining it's gold.

TAKING THE STANCE OF RESCUER

The one playing rescuer is also living an avoidance strategy. By focussing on everyone else's needs and offering to carry their baggage, they are unconsciously making themselves so busy with others' stuff that little to no time is left for them to face their own pain, tackle their own lessons and embrace their personal soul work. Though the rescuer convinces themselves they are being a hero by martyring themselves, the awful truth is that the rescuer is actually CRIPPLING the one playing victim!

Again, imagine a toddler just learning to walk. They let go of a piece of furniture and stagger towards the next, but can't quite make it, so they fall with a bump. Now they are crying. What do you do? Well of course you pick them up and give them a hug, then you look them in the eye and say these magic words "You'll be alright" before you **put them down again**. Those words inspire and reassure the toddler. They feel you have seen them and their efforts.They might not yet be at their destination but your comment has confirmed that they are on a journey towards it and that THEY will make it. That you have seen in them the power to ultimately succeed.

Yet the compulsive rescuer does not do this with the adults around them. Imagine what would happen if you picked up that fallen toddler, slung him over your shoulder and carried him forever because you couldn't bear to see him fall again. He would never learn to walk, his legs would become weak and you would be forever burdened with his weight. The compulsive rescuer, in effect, is doing this to the adults in their life that they think they must constantly step in to fix. But the best way to help a person who stumbles is to remind them of their own power, as you would a toddler, and let them get on with it. The rescuer believes they are acting from the kindness of their heart, but the uncomfortable truth is that their motivation comes from their own need to be wanted, perhaps also a need for power. In persistently rescuing, not only are they doing damage and so disempowering the victim but they are also taking control of another person's journey and 'coursework'. It may hurt the rescuer to see someone they care about struggling, but fall and struggle they must, if they are ever going to learn to 'walk'.

To take yourself away from habitual rescuer mode, take a step back and observe the truth of the situation and the deep truth in your motives. That person chose their own lessons and the struggles they needed to go through. Who are you to second guess that on their behalf? Who are you to 'know better' what they need, better than their own soul knows for itself? Who are you to take on that student's coursework and do it for them, thus depriving them of knowledge that will serve them for the rest of their life? By answering these questions you are less likely to become ensnared by the apparent victim.

Basically they need their struggles in order to grow strong. Therefore, the kindest thing you can do for a person whom you observe playing powerless victim is to simply say "I am sure you will work it out for yourself" or "I have confidence you'll know what to do" or even "I am certain you'll figure this problem out" . Thus inspiring the same confidence that you might inspire in a toddler by making it clear you see them as capable and empowered. After all, a gold medalled marathon runner also struggled, staggered and fell learning to walk in their toddler days, didn't he?

Understanding why you became a rescuer is part of your own growth. Many times the motive comes from feeling valueless in your own life so needing to ensure you become indispensable to others, or fear of not being enough to receive love unless you are in some way playing the 'hero'. But that simply is not true, you are as deserving of love as the next person. There is nothing at all you have to do or be in order to deserve love, but simply stand on the Earth, to simply exist. So who is it you are here to rescue? Why it is YOU of course! Or at least, your wounded child pieces from the past.

TAKING THE STANCE OF PERSECUTOR

This is the personality trait that we most like to shun. Surely that is not me, I couldn't be like that. But at times we all fall into the mode of control freak, manipulating, pushing and even resorting to bullying, to get things to go the way we feel they must. Fear has us in it's grip, and it is this fear that makes us blindly unable to see it any other way. It simply HAS to be done like that or the world could come crashing down. The persecutor is (unconsciously) in blind terror that there is no one to take care of things but themselves and if their demands are not adhered to, the outcome will end in disaster.

The Persecutor fears the rug may be pulled out from under their feet at any moment, because there is no responsible adult above them to take care of things. They feel insecure, so they must ensure that everything is in place for safety's sake. They have a sense that others do not know what they are doing and could at any moment cause an accident. They feel unsupported and overburdened by having to carry the weight of the world on their shoulders, so they lash out. Filled with fear and overwhelmed with responsibility and lack of support they start to push others around. They anxiously try to keep control and order, make things happen as they need them to, through whatever means they must, even if it means resorting to shouting, pushing or bullying. Ironically, the problem is they feel all alone, but by behaving in such a dictatorial manner, they push others away still further.

THE TRIANGLE

Since we choose everything on our Earth walk, there are no victims, therefore there are no persecutors and consequently, there is no need for rescuers. Yet in each family we automatically fall into the slot of either Persecutor, Victim or Rescuer.

1. *THE RESCUER* – the saviour, the one who is driven to make it better by saving everyone from suffering.
   Script - "Don't worry, I'll be here for you, I can fix it, I'll sacrifice myself, my time, my health, my energy just for you. I can carry everyone no matter how much it weighs me down".
2. *THE PERSECUTOR* – the controller, the one who has to make everyone dance to their tune.
   Script – "There's only one way to do it and that's my way, and if you don't do it my way there will be consequences, so whatever it takes I will have to bend you to my will."
3. THE VICTIM – the underdog, the one who seems to suffer the most, the powerless one who is pushed this way and that by the whims of others.
   Script - "Why does this always happen to me, its not fair, I can't win, I am always suffering but it's not my fault" .

In 1968 a student of Eric Berne published this drama triangle model as a tool for use in psychotherapy. In his book he describes the typical family triangle, where each player takes on a role. Its easy to spot. In families and often within workplaces individuals take a stance then dance with the stances of the others within that triangle. I am grateful to Stephen B. Karpman for pioneering the following model, which so clearly indicates family triangle dynamics. Do you recognise yourself or any of your family members standing on any of these points?

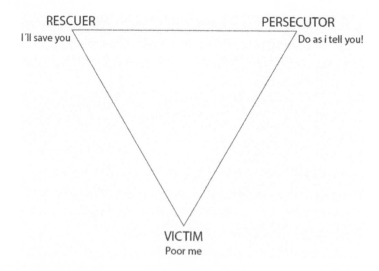

RESCUER   PERSECUTOR

I´ll save you   Do as i tell you!

VICTIM

Poor me

FAMILY DYNAMICS

Each point interacts directly with the other two. Have a little look at your family dynamic, or work environment. Do you see how each person has taken a role? Which one do you play?. Perhaps, at times, you move around the triangle? Sit with each persona for a minute, owning how it is when you live in that skin.

Now here's the interesting game. If you look below the surface of each of the above personas, what do you discover?

So you see, even the persecutor is not a villain, simply another soul struggling to survive, like you. The rescuer is not trying to stifle or steal your power, just needing to be important, and the victim is not a lazy user of others' time and energy, they've simply forgotten their power. Thus, the hidden truth deep within each of these roles, when we scratch the surface, is that they are not quite what they initially seem to be. What we've assumed and have grown used to, and the ways that we have been interacting within these archetypes, is an illusion. Take a closer look at the triangle, and at the labels victim, rescuer and persecutor. Perhaps there is something else entirely going on.

THE VICTIM might in fact be the true **persecutor** or controller.
THE PERSECUTOR might really the true **rescuer** or saviour.
THE RESCUER is might actually be the true **victim** or underdog

Why is this?

THE VICTIM dominates the scene because they rule everyone in the family through their victimhood. They play the 'guilt trip' card to manipulate each member of the group to dance to their tune. So they are masking the fact that they are truly **a persecutor**, pushing everyone into compliance through their emotional blackmail and constant neediness.

THE PERSECUTOR is **the true rescuer**. They are driven to make things better. They are weighed down by a massive sense of responsibility and a fear that there is no one around to make sure everything is alright. If they see a flaw or things not entirely in control, anxiety makes them desperate to correct it. Their rage is driven by terror that everything will end in disaster – they won't get their milk and they're going to die. And they can't die because who else will hold it all together and save us all from dying? Remember, as we said earlier, the soul who offers to play the *bad guy* has made a huge sacrifice. So the persecutor may also be that soul who has agreed to play the *bad* guy to facilitate your learning? Thus, in a strange way, they are rescuing through their challenging behaviour, giving your soul the challenging experiences it has pre-ordered.

THE RESCUER is **the true victim**, as they do not have a life for themselves. Fear and low self-esteem make them a slave to fixing everyone else and every situation. Why? Because they don't believe they have any innate value, don't believe they can be loved unless they step right into the middle of the picture and become an essential hero, even if it kills them.

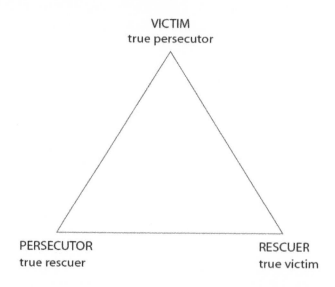

VICTIM
true persecutor

PERSECUTOR
true rescuer

RESCUER
true victim

Once the triangle is set up and everyone knows their role in a family or a group, it becomes a living entity, with everyone slotting into their part and slinking back into their wounds which are provoked by the others in the triangle. When we are immersed in our role within the triangle it is hard to stop our usual knee jerk reactions. So how do we step away from this dance when everyone involved has been practicing the same steps for so long they've virtually worn a groove in the carpet?

The answer is surprisingly simple. Step into the middle of the triangle! Thus you avoid getting caught up in the dramas, but can instead observe. By remaining serene and rational you can watch the player who might have triggered your reaction, notice where they are currently placed on the triangle and know that you can only keep them there by confirming their place through jumping in and dancing the steps with the others in the game, thus keeping it's dysfunction alive. Ignore your natural inclination to take one of the other roles, one that is still up for grabs. Instead, by stepping into the centre, away from the flow, you resist the old well worn emotional involvement. Observe and peel back the layers of each player until you reach the core of their behaviour, FEAR. The fear that they won't get their milk and they're going to die! This way, you see their vulnerability, you remain serene and uninvolved in the game, and your light of compassion and understanding remains at its brightest.

LEARNING TO LISTEN

The most valuable thing in good relationships is the art of truly listening. However, we are so programmed into our adapted roles that we do not realise we are 'blotting out' the person we are meant to be listening to because we've disappeared into our old, knee jerk reaction. This is particularly prevalent if you are a habitual victim or rescuer. The victim will swiftly be lost in their own inner dialogue of 'I'm suffering too'; the persecutor is thinking 'this had better not be my fault, let me point out why it is their fault' and the rescuer is so busy thinking up ways to 'fix' the situation they have entirely stopped listening. They each race to respond without giving the other person the space to be truly seen or heard. When we do this we have gone deaf! When you feel frustrated that the person you wish to talk to is not listening, now you know where they have gone. It is not about you, it is about them and their wounds, and that is where they have disappeared to. If your mind is full of 'how can I fix this' or 'poor me' then there is no room for you to actually listen and truly honour the person who is talking, so there is no space for balanced dialogue. In the next section I will show you a way to become an excellent listener.

HOW TO HANDLE COMPLAINERS

Habitual complainers draw out the rescuer or persecutor in all of us. We want to make it better, we want to fix them, we feel burdened to resolve their problem. So before they've even finished talking we are lost in the inner dialogue of planning how to solve the problem. Both you and the complainer know the steps to this dance, but there is never a solution, because they habitually remain the victim and you habitually remain in the 'trying to rescue or fix, but never quite succeeding' role.

The following technique, originally developed by **Marshall Rosenberg in Non-violent Communication, will take you out of that dance, to enable you to change the old and familiar steps between the two of you. Then, because you have changed your steps, they will be forced to change theirs. This phenomenal technique is healing for all parties, as it lifts you out of the groove you've both been carving through the ages.

What you must do is become a recording device. When you are with this person whether they are your parent, your child, your boss or your partner, decide to pay FULL attention to their actual WORDS rather than the emotion behind them. You will need to be utterly focussed because the name of the game is; you are going to repeat back to them the exact words they have just uttered, verbatim. With no interpreting whatsoever, your job is to give their words back to them neutrally, exactly and unchanged. Think of yourself simply as A RECORDING DEVICE. Here is an example.

Complainer:	"You're always trying to make me do what you want me to do."
You:	"What I heard you say was, that I'm always trying to make you do what I want you to do, is that right?"
Complainer:	"Yes, and you never tidy up after yourself."
You:	"And I heard you say that I never tidy up after myself."
Complainer:	"Yes, and I am tired of always being the one to do the dishes."
You:	"And you are tired of always being the one to do the dishes, is that right?"

You'll be amazed how quickly the situation calms and the complainer settles down. This is for many reasons.

Firstly, you are so busy making certain you have got the words exactly right that you have stepped away from your usual emotional reaction which triggers the habit of searching for a solution. You've become accustomed to not listening while you frantically seek in your mind a way to solve their problem. By following this technique you will block that old emotional response by simply becoming a recording device. Then you are off the hook, you have nothing to fix, no rescuing to do because you will be emotionally and intellectually removed from the old game.

Secondly, their inner wounded child, the one actually doing the complaining, feels truly heard and seen when you give back to them, verbatim, exactly what they just said, which calms them down. Sometimes that's all they have really been craving all along, to be sincerely heard (rather than fixed).

Thirdly, by feeding their own words back to them, they gain clarity and can start to work out for themselves what to do. It is soothing and empowering for both parties. In fact it is game changing. The result will be peace and balance for all.

HOW TO DEAL WITH CRITICISERS

Remember, the person doing the criticising is NEVER talking about YOU. Since the criticism comes FROM them, it is ABOUT them. We all carry shadow pieces, aspects of ourselves we are ashamed of and want to hide, and it is human nature to push these away onto someone else. However, the hilarious truth is, no matter what the shadow piece is, every human being carries that same shadow piece to some degree.

So the next time you receive a criticism, instead of jumping to your own defence or taking umbridge, take a mental step back. Firstly know for sure that deep down inside, that person is fearful that

THEY have this particular trait. It is vital to realise you have nothing to hide, you are neither better nor worse than any other human being. Rest assured that in truth, because every one of us carries every possible negative trait within ourselves, we are all equally flawed, no exceptions. Better than that, we are each exactly perfect just as we are, so long as we are truly doing our best.

Knowing this, you can cease to hide behind what you might consider the acceptable exterior, the nice smile, the polite words, all the while hoping to keep concealed those shadow pieces of yourself that you don't want to own up to, and certainly don't want others to see. Name them, we all have them, laziness, greed, manipulativeness, impatience, resentfulness. The list is goes on. You've been rejecting those aspects of yourself your whole life, we all do it. So they jostle for acknowledgement, hiding behind your back, till one day someone points a finger at you and accuses you of having one of these traits. No, you think, not me, I don't want to own that side of myself, I am NOT that! Then the pressure is laid on, but what would happen if, instead of casting these rejected aspects of yourself out, or trying to hide them, you simply acknowledged and loved them? Those poor, unaccepted and unloved shadow pieces. Life would change hugely for you and your fellow humans.

It takes considerable energy and effort to react with defence against a criticism. The trick to save this energy and gain peace of mind is simple. All you have to do is instantly acknowledge the trait within yourself and love it.

For example, someone says "You know what you are, you are lazy". Well of course you are, somewhere in your being, and though you know your accuser is only offloading onto you their OWN fear of being lazy, you can heal all concerned by simply answering, "Yes I am lazy, and I love that about myself". Or they might say "You are selfish" and you simply answer "Yes I am selfish, and I love that about myself". The critic then has nowhere to go with their criticism. It is not having the desired effect of undermining you, so they stop. Better still, you are unconsciously teaching them that it is ok to love their own hidden shadow pieces.

The fact that the shadow pieces of ourselves that we wish to hide from view, are actually shared by all of humanity, makes it OK to acknowledge and love them. So you've nothing to be ashamed of, nothing to hide. What a joy to embrace every aspect of yourself which in turn will show others how to accept and love every aspect of themselves too. When we cease to run from our inner shadow pieces, we start the process of healing them.

ANGER and AGGRESSION

1. Remember, reasoning will never work if the person is not in control of their faculties. So if they are under the influence of alcohol or drugs, do not get sucked into their delusional dramas. They are not in their right mind and will probably forget the conversation later anyway. Do not waste your energy or your emotions, simply remove yourself from the situation without taking anything they have said personally. Only resume dialogue when they are sober.

2. If someone sober becomes angry, defuse the situation by seeing them as a frustrated child stamping their feet. A child who reacts by lashing out because it does not have the emotional tools to deal calmly with the situation. Thus you must remain calm and mature rather than getting roped into a shouting match between two "toddlers". Faced by anger you need to calmly and compassionately take a mental step back and observe the aggressor and recognise they are truly driven by fear. Answer them neutrally, in balance and without trying to either rescue or fall into the role of victim yourself.

3. If things seem to be escalating towards violence or physical abuse, remain calm and in command of your own emotions. Do not engage. Remove yourself from danger, just walk away. Know that you have the right to your own body, the vehicle for your soul, which no one may violate under any circumstances.

4. If it is you who reacts in an angry outburst, before you reach that stage, take a step away and go within. What is the underlying fear of your wounded child that is provoking such an explosive reaction? The true provoker is not the

object in front of you, it was someone or something from long ago that frightened you when young. Speak with your inner frightened little one, reassure them, then re-enter the scene from calm maturity and wisdom.

Remember, underneath it all, aggression and angry lashing out is not an adult reaction. It is, in fact, an infant or very young child who feels powerless and overwhelmed, ultimately driven by the primal fear that they won't get their milk and they're going to die! Your job is to take care of your self rather than being mesmerised by the need to fix or placate an angry person in your environment And by taking care of your own wounded child you will not fall into the trap of escalating the problem or getting into a fight.

GRIEF

Grief is a personal journey. How many times have you heard, or even thought, "they should be over this by now"? Saying goodbye and letting go does not have a set time frame, it is very individual and the pain can resurface unexpectedly long after the loss. The adjustment may be slow and mournful, or may be intense or numbing, then the person may appear to have moved on. But grieve we must, as humans. To bury our grief only leads to that emotional wound festering under the surface, where it may poison other aspects of our life and body, sometimes years later. Tears and talking are healers, be sincere, allow yourself to mourn and let the grief take its course. Find a good listener, be a good listener. Through the pain of grief we grow, we develop deep empathy and understanding which in turn will help others get through a their own grieving. Here too, it is valuable to cherish your inner wounded child pieces, as they feel the fear of their own mortality in grief situations. Take care of them as you mourn together.

**Marshall Rosenberg, 1934-2015 pioneer of Non-violent Communication*

CHAPTER 5
Love and Partnership

WHAT IS LOVE?

What is love? This is the eternal question. Think about it for a second, what is your definition of love? What is love, for you? My beloved life partner Quinto describes love as 'an exchange of energy with no effort' and for me it is 'thinking with the heart brain instead of the head brain'. Perhaps it is a mixture of both, but whatever your definition it cannot be adequately thought, only adequately felt.

Imagine for a moment that we have more than one brain. The first one, in our head, is rationalising and resolving, it busies itself with duty, organising and strategising. Often it is in overdrive with planning and spends much of its time in the past or in the future, going back over things or thinking ahead, sometimes idealising, imagining or binding itself up in worry or negativity.

The second brain is in our gut. It is filled with microbes that are highly intelligent. So we had better pay attention to our gut feelings. From here came our original food or sustenance, through the umbilical cord. When given an option or asked for a decision it is wise to listen to your gut's response. Listen for an "ah-ha" (yes) or "uh-huh"(no), then follow that rather than your overly influenced, programmed and somewhat controlled brain. As your gut stores emotional intelligence, it is the home of your powerful intuition. Thus, for true clarity in decision making, it is best to delve into your gut feelings.

The third brain is within our heart, that brain holds no fear, no guilt nor criticism. The heart brain is generous, tender, kind, compassionate and unafraid. It flows beautifully as it knows only love. That is why love, for me, is thinking with the heart brain.

Quinto's description of love as an exchange of energy with no effort has been arrived at from observing our greatest teacher, nature. Trees and plants naturally release oxygen for our use and absorb the carbon dioxide, essential for them, which we release. This exchange between the plant kingdom and the human kingdom happens naturally and is thus a loving co-operation and free flowing gift with no effort, demands or expectations.

You feel this when you find yourself walking in the forest or out in nature. Your senses come alive and you are revitalised, your heart opens, you sigh with pleasure, drawing in more oxygen and releasing positive energy with carbon dioxide. You feast your eyes on the beauty and gifts before you. You breathe in life, the smell of fresh earth, damp leaves, wildflowers and feel the warmth of sunlight or soft rain on your skin. Surely this is love being received into you and being sent out from you, joyfully shared giving, happening spontaneously with no sense of sacrifice or consciousness of making an effort to do something for the other. In that moment you are just being your true and authentic self, living in the present moment, thinking with your heart brain, loving the vistas nature has provided. This exchange of energy with no effort happens as with all authentic exchanges, because it is motivated by the natural joy of simply being. Nature's bountiful giving is a wonderful example of what love is. Love without judgement, love without ulterior motives, love without games of victim or rescuer, a pure and simple, open and free sharing.

Nature tirelessly teaches us about love. The Shamans from Peru recommend that at every possible opportunity we walk barefoot on the earth. They also recommend we kiss the earth. Because in our feet and in our lips, are receptors and extraordinarily sensitive sensors which can read and tune into the acidity, minerals and vibrations of our environment, helping us to adjust to wherever we happen to be and to be in good relationship with our surroundings. In adapting and synchronising with the place we are in, we feel a greater balance, a greater truth, we come back home to ourselves and are thus able to express our authentic vibration back out into the universe. Then we can walk in a loving symbiosis with all that is around us.

THE LAW OF ATTRACTION

Coming back home to ourselves and expressing our authentic vibration out, we naturally attract those who fit with us, are in sympathy with our being and can share with us a symbiosis with no effort. That is how you attract the mate who resonates and harmonises with your own natural vibration. Nothing contrived, no effort, you are just being your true self, connected inwardly and outwardly. Like a magnet, you will then attract the person who perfectly synchronises with you, the person whose jigsaw puzzle piece fits perfectly alongside yours, to make the picture work.

In order to reach that state of authentic vibration it is essential that you let go of the fears in your life and move away from all the chatter of your head brain, instead living in the present moment and listening to the heart brain. It is easiest to do this when immersed in nature. When you reach out to connect with your environment, with the earth you walk upon, the plants you eat, with the clouds or stars you gaze at, the air and the water you can be immersed in, the sun and the moon illuminating your world, you remember who you truly are and feel awed by the endless support and love offered by your natural environment. Feeling surrounded by love your heart stays open. Then you can go deep within to connect to your truth, to your real self, your own nature, and realise how your inner and outer worlds are making a beautiful and perfect dance of loving interaction. Your head brain, rationalising and analysing, no longer dominates, but all three brains, head, heart and gut, are synchronised within and without. It is in this moment of balance that you realise you are whole and you are safe and in no need of a 'saviour'. It is at this moment, needing no-one to complete you or fix you, truly content with and connected to who you really are, that a matching soul, the person who genuinely fits with YOU and your vibration, is suddenly and easily by your side.

As we are living in a physical body that follows physical laws, in order to re-connect to it we must re-embrace the physical environment in which we live. However, in the modern world it is all too easy to become disconnected. This long chain of disconnection has been occurring in humans since we ceased living outdoors, where we were in a dance of life with the creatures and plants, seasons and weathers of our natural environment. Nowadays we shut ourselves away in the artificial atmosphere of a car, an office, a house, a college, a hospital. There is no connection with the physical natural elements of which our body, our very breath, is composed.

In living a closed-in life, detached from what is real, we have become divorced from our our true nature. We have forgotten that we are not separate from the natural world but are an essential part of it, flowing with it's laws and gifts every moment of every day. We seldom touch our bare feet on the ground, we take for granted the oxygen in our breath, rarely gaze in awe at the stars and planets that circle our heads each night and of which we are a part. Turn back, reconnect to wonder once again by walking in quiet contemplation in nature, by touching the earth, the grass, the water. Come back to yourself and remember who you truly are, by letting your heart burst with awe and gratitude for the generosity and abundance that surrounds you every single day. You are an essential part of that dance of beauty and abundance because it, and you, are love.

WHAT PREVENTS LOVE

In answer to "Why can't I find love" you've probably been given the answer "First you have to love yourSELF", but that just leaves you scratching your head saying "how?"

The one thing that blots out love is fear, and fear comes about when we believe we are powerless. Yet to be powerless is not our true state, it is an illusion. We have collected that concept, and picked up fear, upon incarnation, because at that point we forgot how supremely powerful we are. But if you could go back and remember who you were before you incarnated, you would remember your power and know that you have nothing to fear, certain that each and every one of us is naturally caring and balanced, a being of love. You release fear and re-embrace your full power of love when you reconnect to your physical body and to the natural environment which carries your support network.

You are a being of love, yet on incarnating, a separation occurred between your innate loving self and the adapted self struggling to survive on this planet. By spending time in nature and in the present moment, you can remember the original loving you and become whole again. When you start to see where fear has been taking over in your life and when you master those fears you can return to love. Only then are you ready to be a partner to another whole and integrated, self loving human being.

Without being connected and in harmony with our environment and thus with our true self, but instead driven by fear and confusion, how can we hope to be in a balanced and loving relationship with anyone else? The way to find happiness in a relationship is to build a strong and balanced relationship with yourself and remembering that fear is just an illusion. Be compassionate, kind and non-judgemental towards yourself, recognising when you feel insecure or imperfect and reminding yourself that you are no less and no more than any other living person because you are perfect exactly as you are.

Now that you are here on Earth, travelling in a human body, respect that body. This is the vehicle that carries your soul and upon which you depend every day, so loving and taking care of it is an integral part of loving yourself. Another way to become disconnected from love, from yourself and from your power, is to eat food that is disconnected, food with which you have no energetic or visual relationship. It is best if you can connect with the source of your food. If you don't observe those veggies growing in the soil, or know the animal from which you get your milk, you are divorced from the source. In today's world many of us consume only the end product that we buy in the store. We don't tend our food and watch it grow, we don't see the source of our water nor where it has been. Some children in the inner city only know that a carrot comes from the supermarket, they cannot begin to imagine it actually growing in earth somewhere outdoors nor imagine a cow being milked. There is no comprehension of the energy of the sun co-operating with the fecundity of Mother Earth to grow all that will grow us. That co-operation between the sun, the Earth, the water and the wind is a clear example of love. And it is this co-operation and love that builds the cells of all that we are, our food and drink become our bodies and our brains, our hearts and our guts. We are beings of love, made from love, surrounded by love on this planet. If we put junk into and disrespect our sacred body and our fertile mind, then we give ourselves yet another hurdle to overcome in re-claiming and re-balancing our truly loving selves.

Reconnect with and truly honour your body, your cells and their genuine requirements. There are ways you can connect to nature even when you live in an apartment in the city. Even if you have no garden, grow some herbs or sprout some seeds on the windowsill. Not only will you be in relationship with the food but it will be fresh, vital and alive. Wherever you are and whatever your circumstances, you can also always energetically connect through gratitude. Each time you eat, be conscious of the life giving energy, send a loving wave of gratitude all the way down the line, from the items of food on your plate to every one who has contributed to that food being there; from the check out girl in the supermarket, to the delivery person, to the picker, the grower, of course the plant itself and ultimately the elements that sustained it, which now sustain you.

Knowing what we need and from what our cells are composed, then ensuring that we put only this best fuel into our vehicle our beautifully designed engine can function at its optimum level, we give ourselves the best chance of living in the vibration of love. It is hardly surprising that in this modern urban world when we are separated from all that is natural, where often we put into our bodies and minds fuel that not only is less than optimum, but also may be intentionally toxic, such as with alcohol or drugs, we lose our authentic vibration in tune with the planet, we lose our Light, our sense of relationship, our sense of self, and become disconnected from who we truly are. Yet it is only when we live in tune with our body and mind's true needs that our Light and vibration can shine out to the world and call in the matching Light and vibration in the form of a soul mate or perfect partner, and put us in right relationship with all our relatives.

You do not need someone else to tell you how wonderful you are, but it feels so good to be praised, admired and appreciated. When this happens it serves as a reminder of your beauty, your talent and your brilliance. Yet all those things were there before the praise came, you just weren't able to embrace and acknowledge them. Now someone else sees these treasures in you it is easier to see them in yourself. Self-criticism and beating yourself up for imperfections is abusive to your soul. Gone are the days when self-abuse was considered a way to get closer to God. In fact it has the opposite effect, keeping you far from tenderness, love and joy.

So, the key to loving yourself starts with remembering you chose to come to Earth and experience being human, bringing your unique set of talents and abilities with you. In remembering that you are supremely powerful you can start to reflect and applaud yourself, sincerely appreciating your own unique traits and gifts, your gold. Patting yourself on the back for how you have overcome challenges, how you have expressed your talent, what you have so far learned and where you have helped others helps you to remember you are a lovable, open-hearted human being. And when you achieve this, it also teaches those around you to accept and love themselves.

IS FEAR blocking A RELATIONSHIP?

Is love a sharing with another human being on all levels, or is love the passion you feel when you see a glorious sunset? Perhaps it is both as the law of attraction is in operation in both cases, so your heart and soul are moved and there is love.

So often a client sitting in front of me will bemoan the fact that he or she cannot find "the one". They wonder why they have been single for so long, and in most cases there are only two things stopping them. Either they have an invisible barbed wire fence or glass wall of protection that they have put up, which surrounds and insulates them from any potential relationship, or they are not vibrating in their own authentic frequency, and are thus divorced from themSELVES. Often it is both.

It is, of course, impossible to get close to someone who has barricaded themselves in, behind a wall. Yet I find so often that the person who has put up this barrier has no awareness of having done so. Only when I point this out does their face show a dawning realisation that indeed they have been hiding behind an impenetrable shield, while all the time declaring "I want to meet someone". The truth is that fear and previous hurts have made them hide. Thus, not only are they frustrated and longing for connection with someone, but they are also exhausted from having to maintain this barrier against intimacy. The wall, constructed through fear of being hurt, let down, getting it wrong again is an manifestation of feeling vulnerable and disempowered. Ironically, the person has no idea how supremely powerful they actually are, has not realised that all relationships thus far experienced have been part of their essential curve of learning, but by no means their final destination. They have completely forgotten that they are in control of their own life experiences and indeed are making great progress. By hiding behind a wall they are blocking some of the most enriching experiences they could have, those of relating intimately with another human being, whether it is forever or not. Only by mastering your own fear can you cease to put up a wall of defence and open yourself to the chance of an awesome partnership which, when you are truly ready, will be truly harmonious and synchronised.

We spend our lives trying to adapt, to be something or someone according to what others might want and expect, or perhaps to simply avoid rejection, complaints or criticism. We fear we are not 'good enough' so we *try* to fit in, to emulate others, or suppress parts of ourselves that we believe make us less desirable, less than perfect, ugly or wrong. Then we forge ahead trying to fit into grooves we perceive to be 'acceptable', leaving behind our true self that we have judged as somehow flawed. It's like a train that feels it must jump to another train's track to reach its destination. Of course, the result is a train wreck. Have you ever experienced a relationships that resulted in an emotional train wreck? Now you know why. Because you felt you were less than perfect.

Here is how that game goes. Imagine for a moment that you meet someone who you fear will not fully accept you exactly as you are, so you put on the good, likeable face while hiding those parts of yourself you think might not be lovable enough. You start to wear this mask in order to be accepted and to be loved. What happens, then, if your partner declares their love for you. The game is on. You know that you are not showing or being your true self, thus they do not REALLY love YOU, they only love the mask. This is how the "I am not lovable" mantra becomes a self fulfilling prophecy. So don't be tempted to wear a mask of what you see as lovable or acceptable. Take the fence down and be one hundred percent your real self, warts and all. Then you can be sure that the person who declares their love for you genuinely loves YOU.

Humanity is a huge and magnificent jigsaw, in which you are one piece. Your particular and unique shape, design, colour, pattern is absolutely perfect to make the picture work. The trouble starts when you don't know or believe this so you carve off a bit here and paint a bit on there, making yourself a different shape or colour.

We try to change ourselves to emulate someone else's jigsaw piece, someone we see as successful or better than us. This effort to fit in and be like our heroes is especially strong in the insecure teenage years. In not fully embracing and accepting who we truly are, we try to suppress bits of our personality, change our natural looks with styling, make up or even surgery.

Remember, you are one perfect piece of the jigsaw puzzle of humanity, just as you are. The trouble is, when you change one piece of the jigsaw puzzle, the whole picture is ruined, then there is a sense of incompletion, we keep searching for the place where we can settle and fit. But it was always there, all we had to do to truly fit in in this world was to love and accept our own original, unique and perfect piece of the puzzle.

In order to love and accept who you are, to be authentic and confidently love your imperfections, embrace the fact that you truly are PERFECT just as you are. You are the best, so you deserve the best, and you can have the best, once you master fear and remember who you sincerely are, deep down inside. The more you grow in compassion and love for yourself, the brighter your beautiful Light shines.

KEYS TO HEALING THE WOUNDS THAT KEEP YOU ISOLATED

In both of the above cases, fear is the driving factor. Fear keeps us running. Running in circles searching for a mate while running away from the risk of finding the wrong one, then running from commitment or running around trying to keep the relationship going. That is as emotionally exhausting as it sounds. So here are the keys to clearing away what has been blocking you, and confidently living your true energy, vibrating at the frequency that will attract the perfect mate.

1. How to let the barriers down safely

The wall or fence you have put up is caused by fear. You have forgotten how supremely powerful you are, because you have forgotten that you can manifest whatever you want. You can get your own milk! The exercise in the next chapter teaches you how to master and overcome all fears. Once you are back in your power and have mastered your fears you will not need to maintain any barrier or fence nor keep your heart locked away ever again. And once you have mastered my technique for taming the dragon, fear, all relationships you have in all aspects of your life will be magically enhanced.

2. How to vibrate in your authentic frequency

The first step is to stop running away from, but go deep and turn towards your deepest self, with true compassion and acceptance. We are so critical of our looks but as I have grown older I have realised that each time I look back over photos of myself taken when I was younger, I think "I looked pretty good back then". Yet back then, at the time when the photo was taken, I remember being quite critical of how I looked. Now I have reached the stage of the wise elder I know for sure that whatever age we are, we are actually just right, but foolishly blind to our own perfection.

So the trick is, in your mind's eye, race ahead to 10 or 20 years from now, then look back and realise that you are great, just as you are now. This mental trick helps us to love our current physical self instead of constantly trying to correct it, tweak it or run away from it. No inner or outer criticism may be allowed to contradict the fact that you are designed to be perfect just as you are, right now. No more hiding behind a mask of acceptability, it is time to trust you are truly lovable exactly as you are. If you think you have flaws it helps to realise that to a greater or lesser extent, EVERYONE carries those same flaws within them, and we are each unique yet perfect.

DECODING YOUR CURRENT RELATIONSHIP

Take a look at these components. Are any of them present in your current relationship?

INSECURITY
LONGING
NEED TO CHANGE YOUR PARTNER
NEED TO SAVE YOUR PARTNER
NEED THEM TO FIX YOU
NEED THEM TO KEEP YOU SAFE
DEPENDENCE
BETRAYAL
CONTROL
HEARTBREAK
STRIVING TO BE GOOD ENOUGH
LOSS OF POWER
SUBSERVIENCE
VICTIMHOOD
ABUSE

If your relationship contains any of the above, then love is blotted out by fear and you are being alerted to the need to work with your own wounded child (method in Chapter 7). You are being given the signal to support that frightened little one and give them the confidence to speak up for themselves, stand up for their rights, give them a voice.

In any kind of dysfunctional relationship, listen your own voice, if you say 'YOU' did this or 'YOU make me feel' that, be aware that you are not owning your stuff. Learn instead to use the 'I' word. Declare "I feel uncomfortable when you do/say this" or "What I would like is...". By remembering to say 'I' instead of 'you', the relationship will run more smoothly. When we start accusing with the word 'you' we are wasting our breath, because the person we are talking to will have immediately closed their ears. On the other hand, when we use the 'I' word, we can be heard.

However, if physical or emotional abuse is taking place, know for certain that you are worth more than this and simply **walk away**, making it clear that no-one is allowed to steal anything from your body or soul. Thus you take the first step to regaining your confidence and power, which may have been undermined to keep you trapped in a dysfunctional and dangerous pattern.

I THOUGHT HE/SHE WAS THE ONE

How many times have I heard the complaint "I thought he/she was the one, why did it all go wrong?" When we come out of a failed relationship we may feel hurt, with a loss of confidence in our own ability to make the right decisions, especially about relationships. But in that moment you have forgotten that everything is unfolding exactly as you pre-planned it, there are no mistakes, only opportunities for growth and learning.

You shake your head and nurse your broken heart wondering how it could have seemed so right at the beginning, yet gone so wrong at the end. Yet, all that has really happened is that YOU have attracted into your life the very issues that you are needing to clarify and resolve. The profoundly heart-rending experiences that, deep down on a soul level, you are striving to learn from. You are not wrong, you have made no mistake, your judgement remains sound, do not fret. You are still on track, you have placed yourself in the perfect situation to achieve great learning from that relationship, its beginning and its ending.

So here is an interesting exercise to help you gain perspective with regard to what went on in a failed relationship. Take a sheet of paper and draw a line down the middle. Make two columns with the following headings.

Left hand column WHAT I FELL IN LOVE WITH ABOUT HIM/HER. Right hand column WHAT WERE THE HORRIBLE THINGS ABOUT HIM/HER.

Start by writing a list in left hand column, as you cast your mind and heart back to the first flush of romance, remember the magic and jot down words to describe the glory of that sublime person whom you adored. It might start something like this...

Funny
Beautiful
Sexy
Clever
Kind

and so on. When that is done, start filling the column on the right with the negatives about that same person whom you thought you loved but who broke your heart. It might look something like this...

Unreliable
Selfish
Controlling
Unkind
Cruel

In the next section I will show you what your lists really mean, and what you discover will surprise and illuminate you, showing what this deeply enamoured **falling in love** was really about.

"FALLING" IN LOVE

When we fall in love we lose all our boundaries and go into an altered state. Everybody wants to be loved, and since we are now human, we seek it from other humans. When we incarnated we disconnected from Source, and we miss being immersed in unconditional love. Now we search for that divine love in other humans, but each of **them** is also disconnected from Source.

Clutching at the hope that this person or that person can connect us, or that they can replace the nurturing aspects of our parents when we were little, only leads to disappointment. Yet we don't have a clue that this is what we are actually seeking as we fall head over heels in love.

Let us look at the lists you just made. First we will look at the column on the left, all the fabulous things you fell for in that person. It is time to take on board that the list of great attributes are actually all beautiful aspects of your own personality and character that you haven't believed in, nor had the confidence to embrace.

Read that list again, only this time breathe in all the magnificent things you have written and allow yourself to accept that you embody each one, they are yours! Now you can recognise that you were searching for them in someone else simply to see a reflection of yourSELF in the mirror of that person. Read that list for a third time and bathe in the glory that all of those magnificent things are a true part of your essence, and love them.

Now for the list on the right It may surprise you to learn that the list on the right represents the negative aspects of one of your parents, your mother or your father, the things that triggered pain from them and fear in you when you were a child. After going through this exercise I hope you are feeling less grief or blame about the end of that relationship, instead seeing that the perfection you were looking for is already within YOU!

THE PURPOSE OF FAILED RELATIONSHIPS

When you incarnated you took on the mantle of a helpless and dependent being. This was true on a physical level and you developed the consciousness that your very survival depended on the support of your parents so you programmed yourself that at all costs, you must keep them strong. Thus you grew up fearful of losing them and eternally trying to fix or save them. Your own sense of powerlessness as a child and this need to rescue your parents left many unanswered questions and much unfinished business, which stunted your emotional growth.

So it is that, as an adult we actually seek out a partner who will behave similarly to the negative and style cramping aspects of that parent. By aligning yourself to this particular partner you bring yourself back to the same challenges that caused many of your childhood wounds. This time it is the person you have chosen to team up with, instead of your parent, who confronts you with that same insurmountable negative energy. You do not see it at first. In fact this person may seem very different from your parent, yet as time goes by this new love of yours becomes the one who will replicate the behaviour of your wounding parent. On a very deep and unconscious level you had sensed all along that this person carried those traits of your parent, and thus the relationship would be a perfect fit, for the learning and growth you had to do.

Off you went into the world with your radar scanner, totally unaware that you were seeking a parent replica to "fall in love" with, for your soul's growth. Then 'ding, ding, ding', off goes the scanner. At first it may seem you have found someone very different from your wounding parent, but on a deep level your soul has recognised this person will develop those same traits later in the relationship.

This is "THE ONE" you decide "I feel as if I've come HOME". Well you have indeed come home, to your childhood home! You've come home to the energy of the parent or authority figure you couldn't cope with. You have found the same disappointments and hurts though you don't realise this when you decide to team up with them.

Yet you have done this with the express purpose of completing your growth in order to reach your potential.

As if you were a lopsided tree that had only matured on one side due to a restriction that kept the other side stunted, you feel a need to stretch outwards and upwards, pushing against that restriction to achieve your full height and breadth. Your soul knows that you must identify the block, and empower yourself to overcome its restriction, in order to reach your full glorious and expanded stature. So you choose this partner to place the same blocks in your way, creating the same restrictions for you to push against, overcome and grow beyond. This partner is replicating the obstacles to your growth that your parent placed in your path, thus this partner has come into your life with a purpose – to teach you how to calmly and maturely grow towards and overcome those restrictions you experienced in your childhood.

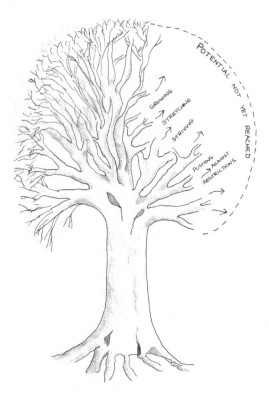

Now, as a wise adult you have the maturity, the vocabulary and the tools to push and strive towards that margin and break through into the light. The method to do this will be revealed in Chapter 7.

In selecting a partner who shows the same negative characteristics as your parent, you give yourself the opportunity to find new ways to address that issue and overcome it, to stand up for the wounded part you carry within yourself and give the wounded child a voice. Thus pushing your branches of growth out towards the restriction until you reach full height and breadth, emotionally.

For example, if a parent was domineering when you were little, you would choose to marry someone who could do the same until it reached the point where you were able to speak your truth out clearly, "Your domineering way is not acceptable to me" or "When you try to dictate to me or control me I feel uncomfortable, unheard and diminished, therefore I do not wish to be treated in this manner, I deserve to be given full respect and appreciation". The marriage usually ends there, when the matured self speaks up for the vulnerable wounded child within, job done!

When you choose someone who replicates that repression you experienced from your parent, you are on a journey of healing that will end in success for you and completion for the relationship. When the healing and necessary soul growth has occurred within that relationship, there is an ending, a separation, a divorce. It is complete, no more work to do on that wound. Then it will be time to move on with gratitude for the learning and liberating opportunity it brought you. So rather than mourning the loss of the relationship, wouldn't it be empowering to see the brilliant purpose it has served and how it has facilitated your growth and the reclaiming of your lost power.

One of the most fascinating aspects of astrology is that it is possible to compare two charts and see what the dynamic of their relationship is. It is possible to see whether two people are compatible on an energetic level or whether the partner they have chosen actually represents their parent rather than their partner. It shows clearly when the partners have unconsciously chosen someone who can replicate their father or mother's negative traits, rather than a life partner.

As children we do not have the knowledge, the words nor the confidence to challenge our parent, to stand up and declare clearly that we do not feel comfortable with their treatment of us and insist that they back off. We simply absorbed it and stored it away. We were wounded and unable to solve the problem or stop the hurt. But in adulthood we have the tools, or can develop them.

That is why we partner with someone who will bring to the surface the fears and emotions from the past. It is done completely unconsciously and the attraction is usually very strong indeed. Such relationships serve their purpose. The sooner you can realise that is what your relationship has been about, the sooner you can heal those old wounds and move on.

I was with a client who was not very happy with her husband. I analysed their charts and saw clearly she had chosen not a partner but someone who energetically and behaviourally replicated her father. When I pointed this out she said "No, he's nothing like my father". To which I replied "OK, so what was the most upsetting thing about your father". She thought for a moment and said "That he was never there, was always travelling and unavailable". Then I asked her "And what is the most upsetting thing about your husband?" Suddenly she stopped, eyes widened and she got it "Oh my goodness, he's never there, he's totally unavailable". I was then able to explain to her that she had selected this partner because he gave her the chance to give a voice to her inner wounded child. I then asked her what that little girl would have said to her dad if she had had the wisdom, the vocabulary and confidence to stop the pain. Then she understood. She knew what she must say to her husband, in order to give that sad little girl her voice. It wasn't going to be easy. She felt trepidation at stepping into the unaccustomed place of standing up for herself and declaring her needs, to say to her husband "I am not comfortable with you being absent so much, I feel sad when you are away because I miss you and I would like it if you could spend more time WITH me, be more available, share more with me as my companion". Whew! The relief that came over her when she actually did it! She realised it was what her little girl self had needed to say all along, to clear away those old wounds.

She took her courage back home and spoke up for herself and this had a remarkable effect. By stepping out of the old dance they had been in for so long as a couple, she automatically triggered her husband's growth as well. It doesn't always work this way. If he was not ready to grow, he would not have complied with her request and she would have been the only one to learn from this transition. But that would not represent a failure, because the purpose ultimately is not to change our partner but to heal ourself, to clear old wounds and grow the stunted part of ourselves into blossom and fruition. It takes courage, but the inner child work in Chapter 7, is key to achieving true fulfilment.

Once that partnership dynamic has run its course you may go through one or two more relationships to heal different aspects of parental wounds until you reach that magical state of being - true contentment with your authentic self, with no need to seek out anybody to fill gaps in you. Then you are ready to shine your true and sincere Light out into the world completely at ease with being with yourSELF in your own company.

When you live your life content to be YOU and following your own dreams and gifts, without a partner to complete you or fix you, that is when the person who perfectly synchronises with your true energy appears, and love finds you! Then you will be in a true partnership, the kind that often begins calmly as a friendship, without all the bells and whistles. A deep compatibility which develops into a lifelong contentment, simply an acceptance of each other exactly as you each are. Then you will be thinking with your heart brain as there will be a natural exchange of energy that will happen with no effort.

When you NEED no one, you will meet someone who is equally content within themselves and the dynamic will be a lasting one of two wise, empowered beings choosing to share a life as equals with no need to save or be saved. No one is ever going to come along and save or fix you and you have no job to save or fix another person either. The co-operative sharing of two equals with no hidden agenda is the ideal partnership, only achievable when each individual has the wisdom and maturity to fearlessly steps into and manifest their true self.

When we are searching for that elusive love in another person, could it be that it is the love from Source that we truly miss and are searching for in another human being, the Light of unconditional love from whence we came? In order to be truly happy it is vital that you make your OWN connection to the Source, fill your soul with that Light, remember how good it feels. Most of us look elsewhere, we try to track it down in another person whom we hope will bring us back to that space of love we long for. But it is too much to ask another human, struggling on their own path, to be the replacement for that loving Light which was your original home. The only way to re-enter that state of being unconditionally loved and bathed in Light, is to plug directly into the source yourself. You can achieve this on a daily basis through meditation or by practicing the Daily Alignment detailed for you in the following chapter.

We are homesick, but we look in the wrong direction for the connection we long for. By choosing to come here we took on a phenomenal learning opportunity, but to make it indelible we agreed to forget where we came from and what we set up for ourselves. There is a deep ache for 'home', and we search for it in all the boyfriends/girlfriends we meet, until (and here is the cosmic joke) we look inside and find that in fact that Light we have been searching for dwells within us, and can be topped up from Source through prayer or meditation. Only then can we feel truly whole or settled with any partner. Wisdom comes with maturity and many older folks who have had enough glimpses along life's way, and the benefit of countless years of life experience, layer upon layer of learning, remember who they truly are and are able to settle back into themselves contentedly, without that eternal longing. Life without unquenched longing and without hampering fear is smooth, joyful and beautiful. Sharing that life with another fearless, natural and truly awakened soul is spectacular.

CHAPTER 6
Your Daily Alignment

AN ESSENTIAL MEDITATION FOR PROTECTION AND CONNECTION

This daily meditation will rebalance you, fill you with love and keep your aura or luminous body clean. We humans are like walking trees, we have branches that stretch up and roots that reach down, yet we spend so much of our waking time just conscious of what is directly in front of us. We are perpetually bombarded by the frequencies and energies of our environment and by other humans dwelling on the planet with us. This can cause us to feel constrained, out of tune and and unable to move in harmony with our environment.

When I encountered The Light in my near-death experience, I knew I had come home to the Source. To be bathed in that Light of absolute, totally unconditional love is beyond blissful. On our daily Earth walk there is a part of us that always misses the profundity of that original source of love and it is easy to get trapped in the search for that same perfect love in another human. From time to time we glimpse it here or there in someone, when their Light truly shines. But they are, like us, also a 'student' at this University called Earth, and they too are yearning for the Source of divine love. We all possess an inner longing that may never be satisfied until we learn to re-connect with that Source, the Light of unconditional love, while we are still here on Earth.

So I offer here this beautiful, simple yet profound meditation, to bring back your connection with The Light and with your own core of Love. It restores and resets you back to calm, love-infused balance. I call this meditation the Daily Alignment. It is the way in which you can recharge your Light by 'plugging' back into the Source, rather like plugging into mains electricity to recharge your battery and illuminate your world. By practicing this simple alignment each morning, you will be filled with Divine Light and reminded of your truth, your essence and your connections while deterring unwanted influences or depletions.

The Daily Alignment was inspired by a beautiful wise elder and friend, *Ingrid, who many years ago shared profound teachings and ceremony with me. I thank her every day for her inspiration and her beautiful soul. Those teachings, plus direct downloads, have inspired this Daily Alignment I offer to you now. For the many seekers I have shared it with over the years, it has turned out to be an incredibly profound daily repair and reconnection practice. It has inspired, helped and healed so many over the years that I am now honoured and delighted to pass this deep yet simple technique on to you.

Following the instructions below, you will notice that I use the word "aho". This is a short version of the beautiful Lakota phrase "aho, mitakuye oyasin" meaning all my relations or we are all one. It is traditionally spoken during prayer and ceremony, to include, acknowledge and honour all relatives, including our guides, ancestors, angels, ourselves and the spirits in all things. With deep respect and gratitude to the Lakota people for this magical and empowering phrase, I invite you to use it's short form 'aho' whenever honouring the divinity within all creatures and things. We are all connected, separation is an illusion. WE ARE ONE FAMILY....AHO.

To do this meditation daily is life-changing. Many of my clients, no matter what their challenge, from grief to addiction, from shame to anger, confusion or loss, have been able to heal completely through practicing this Alignment.

It has so many benefits, including strengthening your natural luminous body or aura and protecting you from pollutants, both energetic and physical. It has healed and helped so many, now it is your turn.

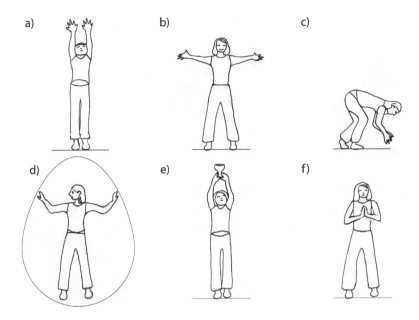

Firstly, honour the four compass directions in a simple way.

1. Start by facing **east** and raise your arms saying "Honouring the spirits of the east, the sunrise, the dawn, springtime, the freshly-planted seed, my yellow brothers and sisters, teachers, healers and guides. Honouring the element of air and the mental aspect of myself. Aho!"

2. Turn to face the **south**, raise your arms saying "Honouring the spirits of the south, the mid-day sun, summertime, the ripe harvest, my black brothers and sisters, teachers, healers and guides. Honouring the element of fire and the physical aspect of myself. Aho!"

3. Turn to face **west**, raise your arms saying "Honouring the spirits of the west, the sunset, the autumn, time of reflection, my red brothers and sisters, teachers, healers and guides. Honouring the element of water and the emotional aspect of myself. Aho!"

4. Turn to the **north**, raise your arms saying "Honouring the spirits of the north, the wintertime, the night-time, time of rest and restoration, my white brothers and sisters, teachers,

healers and guides. Honouring the element of earth and the spiritual aspect of myself. Aho!"

5. Continue turning to face East once more. Raise your arms and with eyes closed turn your face upwards. Go deep, allow yourself to imagine coming face to face with The Light (as I did in my near-death moment). Start to visualise and feel yourself being bathed in that total, unconditional love. Slowly draw that exquisite golden/white Light down through the top of your head. See the glorious Light of unconditional love gradually fill you from the head, down your neck, your arms, your torso, all the way to your toes. (image a.)

6. Now, you are shimmering from head to toe, illuminated with unconditional love. Holding your arms stretched out at your sides, visualise yourself standing on the Earth as an angel of Light, beaming out total, unconditional love in all directions. This feels good! (image b.)

7. Gradually become aware that deep below your feet, Mother Earth's core is a rich red colour. Bend and draw that rich red up through your feet and up through your entire body all the way to the top of your head. (Image c.)

8. As the rich red pours out of the top of your head, it meets the golden/white coming down, to create a beautiful copper colour. Now, with molten copper on your fingertips, define a copper egg all around your body (about an arm's length out) till you are completely encased and protected within that copper egg. (Image d.)

9. It is time for the most important part of this meditation. With the flat of your hands and using your mind's eye, check your copper egg for any gaps, holes, dents or cracks. Then with the molten copper on your fingertips, seal and repair them. Once you have checked and ensured your copper egg is intact, give it a lovely brisk polish all around with your hands.

10. Cup your hands in front of your heart and imagine you are holding a chalice there. This is your own personal chalice so it can be any colour or texture that seems right to you, from plain carved wood to ornate and bejewelled gold.

11. **FIRST** Visualise placing into the chalice **YOUR WHOLE SELF.** Then raise the chalice up to The Light, for love, healing and blessing, arms stretched above your head. *(Image e.)*

12. **SECOND** Bring the chalice down empty, holding it in your cupped hands once again in front of your heart. This time visualise placing into it all of **YOUR LOVED ONES**, one by one. Then raise the chalice up to bring them all to The Light for love, healing and blessing.

13. For the **THIRD** time place the chalice in front of your heart and this time put into it all of **YOUR WORRIES**, all of your troubles, all of your concerns. Now, raising the chalice up to The Light say out loud *"Not mine to take care of, everything to the highest possible good".*

14. For the **FOURTH** and final time, place into the chalice ANYONE WHO has ever upset or **HURT YOU**, from today going right back through your life. Then raise them up in the chalice to The Light, for love, healing and blessing.

15. With arms still raised place palms together in a prayer pose. Touch them to your forehead say out loud *"In truth"*...Then to your heart, saying *"I am". (Image f.)*

16. Very slowly open your hands and as you bring them down to rest beside you, you will notice you are standing in a very different atmosphere from when you started. This sacred space you have just claimed will stay with you throughout the day.

For full benefit to be felt from your Daily Alignment, I recommend you practice it every morning, first thing. It is best to take your time and go deep, but don't worry if you are rushing to get to work or out the door to an appointment, just follow the above steps super fast on those days, which is far, far better than missing a day. I always say if it's a choice between brushing your teeth and doing your Alignment, choose the Alignment (don't tell a dentist I said this!). On days when you have more time you can enjoy the luxury of doing this meditation in a slow, peaceful and profound way. Of the entire exercise the most crucial thing is the maintenance of your copper egg, as this holds your boundaries and deters unwanted influences from entering your personal space, maintaining your equilibrium and integrity, strength and power.

www.Avillion.com

CHAPTER 7
Taming the Dragon – Fear

All of our lives we have left keys along the way, keys to solving the many riddles that confound us today. We race along, so busy looking forward that we don't even notice those precious keys which have grown tarnished, been trodden on and left unclaimed on our path. Yet it is only with those keys that we can unlock the door to our essence, to our happiness, to our power and to the true success of our mission on this planet. It is my joy to show you how to find and polish those keys, so you may unlock any personal doors that you wish to open.

Look again at the image of 'the fear moments' in Chapter 3. Remember, you pick up fear just prior to birth. Then, like a beautiful jewel, each time in your developing life that you experience a fearful moment, a little piece of you breaks off. This fragment is lost in the moment of impact, too stunned to carry on developing with the rest of the jewel. Each of these wounded child pieces remains in the past, yet it can forever haunt the present if something happens to remind you of that original fear or pain. The feelings you experienced way back then are buried deep within you, but can be triggered again and again by difficult circumstances in your current life. Running in the background and prompting unhelpful knee jerk reactions, these old unresolved wounds and fears create imbalance in your daily life and in your adult relationships, right through to old age.

A current disagreement may not seem to have any bearing on your childhood traumas, yet it can rapidly descend into a downward spiral as your inner wounds start to take over. Unbeknown to you or the person you are falling out with, both of you have taken a trip back into the past and are reacting to the emotions held there, in truth, responding as scared and powerless children.

Each frightening experience from about three months before birth, to birth itself and the countless subsequent fearful moments during your childhood - fears of abandonment, fears of failure, fears of being hurt again and so on - all leave a marker. You were young, not yet empowered nor mature enough to handle the situation back then. And all through your early childhood, a plethora of situations occurred that filled you with fear, shame, guilt and other negative emotions. You were in the process of learning to become a wise master of your life, but not yet equipped to deal with those feelings.

What blocks us from achieving the goal of learning and growing our Light brighter now, as adults, is an abundance of these old wounds. The wounded part of ourself and it's accompanying emotions are held, like a freeze frame, in that incident. Then in your present day life, when a threatening or unnerving situation occurs, emotions from an original fearful moment will flood back and drive your reactions, taking you away from the mature and empowered being you are now striving to become.

It is of vital importance to recognise that **ANY emotion that comes up which is not based on love, is ALWAYS coming from fear**.

In trying to make sense of ourselves, our emotions and our relationships, most of us have been searching in the wrong direction for the answers. We have been looking away from the box containing our fears, instead of into it. We've been shying away from the dragon that seems to be one step behind us, instead of turning around and taming it. And the only way to tame the dragon FEAR is by getting to know it, having compassion for it, becoming its friend and reassuring it into calmness. By opening that box and becoming acquainted with the small version of yourself, the one that carries the fears, you can neutralise them and step back into your power. This is the way to truly become the master of your life. Yet how to do this?

I am so happy to share with you the following extraordinary technique, which is absolutely life changing. It is an essential tool which you can use whenever you feel challenged or find yourself moving away from the essence of love back into your childlike state of disempowered fear. I have developed and taught this method to many thousands of people with extraordinary and wonderful results.

YOUR KINGDOM

If you look at your forearm you will see that it is covered with smooth skin, yet under a microscope you would observe that your skin is actually made up of thousands of individual cells which work together to make a cohesive whole. Similarly, the body of humanity is made up of thousands of individual cells, each one an unique and love driven human like yourself. We are each designed to fit perfectly into our role as one vital cell in the body of humanity. Then we become a bunch of essential and dynamic individuals that unite to create the complete and beautifully functioning organism.

You, one of those essential cells in the body of humanity, are supremely powerful. After all, you had the power to choose to incarnate, set up your coursework and even select the actors who would be your challengers and teachers. You had the power to plan all of your major life events and you do have the power to overcome all obstacles. Indeed you have enough power to manifest everything required for your life journey. However, after you made all your choices and put the entire plan into action, your memory banks were wiped so that you would be able to experience everything moment by moment, as it unfolded. From the instant you launched yourself into the state of being human you were set up to forget that it had all been orchestrated by **you**.

If you are reading this book, you have chosen *now* as the time to be reminded of this and are ready to re-collect your power and live in your natural state of love overcoming fear. For that is who you truly are in your essence, a powerful and perfect being of divine love. Love reigns supreme when it comes to power, and love is the counter-point to all other emotions, which are driven by love's opposite, fear.

In my Shamanic tradition, deer represents the power of unconditional love. There is an old Native American legend about fawn, who embodies this love. The story describes how Love is the ultimate, unconquerable weapon, which can simply dissolve any adversary. In Jamie Sams' beautiful Medicine Cards book this legend is described fully. But here is an abbreviated version of the legend... *there was a demon living up the mountain and no one could get past him. He came out of his cave snarling and blocked their way as they tried to go up that trail, up to Great Spirit. Many tried, they armed themselves increasingly, but each time the monster drove them back, no matter what weapons they wielded nor how fiercely they fought. However, one day fawn, eyes filled with love and heart full of compassion for this oversized bully, wandered up the path. The demon was so utterly surprised that all his huffing and puffing, ranting and threats were greeted by an abundance of love and gentleness, that his heart melted, so fawn was able to pass and make her way up the mountain to Great Spirit...*

In this story Deer reminds us to use the power of persistent love and gentleness to touch the hearts and minds of wounded beings. Thus we can melt the demon fear, which would otherwise keep us from our truly sacred, loving selves, and our own connection to Great Spirit. This metaphor shows us a phenomenal truth about conflict, war and aggression. That there is one more powerful weapon than any invented, and that supremely powerful 'weapon' is unconditional love. The gentle and non-judgemental essence of unconditional love stirs in others the memory of their true self and overcomes their own enemy within, fear. And so it is with any imbalance and loss of personal power, the ultimate way to defeat this demon is with loving compassion for ourselves, and more particularly, for those wounded child parts of ourselves that can cause us to act like the snarling demon on the mountain, but in truth are merely afraid. In this chapter I am going to show you how to develop a loving relationship with your own lost soul pieces in order to transmute your inner fear into love.

I am grateful to *Eric Berne and his teachings on Transactional Analysis and to my spirit guides and helpers who inspired me with the following method, explaining how we can find and reclaim those lost fragments of ourselves that broke away, through trauma, so long ago. This is a superb way to bring yourself back into balance, wholeness and power.

Imagine yourself for a moment as one unique cell in the body of humanity. This is your personal kingdom and you are the ruler, or sovereign, presiding over your own individual and private domain. Since we know that you come from love, which is your true nature, you are of course a fine, empowered and benevolent king or queen, in command of your kingdom, governing with, and emanating, love.

Yet, you are not alone there, because within your kingdom are the *peasants* or the frightened, powerless ones. When they are afraid they turn to you, their Sovereign, with their worries, hoping you will hear their pleas and do something about the problem. They look to you, the wise one, the empowered one, to keep them safe because they are frightened and helpless. They cry out to you, *"The castle might be invaded, we're all going to die!"* Or *"There might not be enough food put by for the winter, I am going to starve"*. When they feel vulnerable and filled with fear they need reassurance and support from you, their almighty king or queen who is in charge of their kingdom.

Now, since you are the wise sovereign and hold all the power, you have two choices. You can stop whatever you are doing and pay full attention to the anxious *peasant*, hear what he or she has to say and deal with them in a kind, reassuring manner or you can walk away swiftly, doing your best to ignore those disturbing cries. And here is where we come unstuck, because the majority of humans do not stop to hear and reassure the *peasant,* their own inner wounded child. Instead they turn their back and walk away. After all, they've got things to do, they're busy, they don't want to be bothered!

Perhaps they actually find the *peasant's* cries disturbing, stirring up something they don't want to be reminded of, throwing a curve ball to veer them from their path. Or perhaps they feel they haven't got time for this right now. Either way, they ignore the fearful pleas of the helpless one and march off in the other direction. So many of us do this, yet it leads to a magnification of what could have easily been resolved, because by walking away we start a chain reaction, ultimately resulting in the collapse of our kingdom.

In my long years as a healer it has become evident that all physical, emotional, mental and spiritual ills come from untamed fear and the resulting loss of power. It is a habit we get into, to walk away from nagging doubts and anxieties, hoping to blot out the cries of the our inner wounded child (the *peasant*) by being busy, by getting on with something 'important' in the other direction. We simply don't want to hear them, be bothered by them, be stopped in our tracks when we are rushing forward to the next thing we believe to be essential in our lives. But in so doing, we begin to lose our sovereignty. We go personally out of balance then trigger imbalance in our kingdom and in those around us.

If ignored, the *peasant's* fear escalates. Feeling alone and unheard, this frightened and helpless one grows increasingly anxious. Their voice gets louder as they make a desperate bid for your attention. If you continue to ignore their plight, they feel they must try to take over the kingdom. Unheard, unseen and with no one to reassure and settle them, the peasant panics and makes its way to the control room. It is then that you are triggered to react with an emotion that is driven by fear.

It's not an effective or calm way to run a kingdom, in fact it is chaos. Yet it happens every day in all of our lives, simply because we didn't stop and listen. Simply because we allowed the wounded inner child's fear to rule instead of the calm, assertive, and mature sovereign staying in command.

Remember, in your growing up years, every time there was a trauma, drama or major fear experienced, a piece of you broke away from the precious jewel of your developing being. Each of the frightened *peasants* within your kingdom represents one of those lost and traumatised child pieces of you. Unseen, unsupported and terrified, these wounded children go to pieces, they've nowhere to turn to for reassurance. They're all alone and still there, stuck at the age and in the moment of that traumatic event. They never grew past it and they never moved forward. It is **they** who carry all of your fear.

Without attention and reassurance from you, the wise, mature sovereign, these helpless and isolated ones grow frantic, then overwhelm the kingdom. With you no longer in command and the kingdom taken over by a frightened and inexperienced child, fear rules everything.

How often have you observed a fully grown man or woman acting like a child? It happens all the time and you know you have also reacted in that way. In such moments, the kingdom is lost and the wounded child speaks out of the adult's mouth, trying to drive a vehicle that, due to their desperation and inexperience, could crash at any moment.

Now let us take a further look at your kingdom. I said that you are not alone, as the frightened *peasants* dwell there, but you also have within your kingdom and constantly trying to influence you, the *Advisors To The Throne*. They are your inner critics.

Imagine for a moment that you are a king or queen, the president or ruler of your country and that you have employed some advisors whom you can call on for a mature point of view, for an opinion, or some wise counsel when you need it. They purport to be there to help and guide you, their ruler. They could whisper such things in your ear as, *"Don't forget to look both ways before you cross the*

road'. However, more often you'll hear them whisper criticisms and negative comments, which gradually undermine you, such as "You are a waste of space". That is because they actually have a secret agenda, they want to take over the kingdom, YOUR kingdom.

You only signed them up for wise counsel and support, yet given the chance they'll bring you down and start to rule. The way in which they do this is through criticism. So it is the advisors you hear whispering negatively in your ear. They are the voices of shame and blame, your confidence busters. These advisors can sabotage and disturb you with comments such as, "*You're not good enough*" "*What do you think you're doing?*" "*You got that wrong again didn't you?*", "*You're useless*", "*You're a failure*". How loud and insistent they are! We are mesmerised by their finger wagging criticisms and soon they start to blot out all other, more positive thoughts! They very cleverly and successfully hook straight into your inner fears, bypassing you and talking directly to your insecure *peasants* *(*frightened child pieces*)*. Again, you can lose your kingdom, this time to be run by a deadly combination of frightened children and conniving advisors (critical parents), who will escalate the peasants' fears in order to get you off the throne.

Anarchy and chaos ensues as you react from your inner *peasant* helplessness and timid fearfulness but then swing into the opposite reaction, your critical advisor makes you harangue and finger point. Does this ring a bell? Isn't this exactly what happens when people start to fight? It's dysfunctional chaos, and it has one starting point, the ignoring of the *peasants* when they turn to you for help in the first place.

The whole kingdom falls into disarray when the frightened *peasants* are not listened to and reassured. They get louder and more insistent, which triggers the the advisors to react with "Now's our chance, we can muscle in and take the kingdom for ourselves". They stir up a riot, feeding the insecurity and anxiety of the helpless ones with comments such as, "*Yes, there's going to be an invasion, you will starve, no one will protect you, no one sees you, no one loves you,*

you are all alone and you'll probably die because you are not worth it, you are of no value, you are powerless and not good enough!"

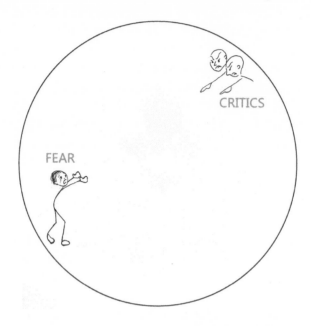

Where is the king or queen? Out of the picture. The takeover has succeeded. In frantically swinging from helpless frightened *peasant* to dominant and controlling advisor, everything has gone haywire. This kingdom in chaos desperately needs the return of its serene, balanced and empowered king or queen, YOU. What started with you turning away from your helpless peasant and paying attention to the dominating critics, has resulted in your complete disempowerment.

This dysfunctional loss of the kingdom is common in us humans, leading to all the unloving reactions such as anger, frustration, resentment, sadness, in fact **all emotions that are not love**. Yet most of us lose our kingdoms more than once on a daily basis, even if we don't always show it externally. We judge, first of all ourselves, then others; we allow fear to creep in, then unloving feelings come up that haunt us. No wonder we're in a mess. Where is that stately and benevolent energy which can keep the kingdom productive and at peace? Where is the sovereign, our own calm and wise essence of pure love, our divine and empowered self?

It doesn't stop there. When we are out of balance, we provoke an out of balance reaction in the people around us. When your reactions to events are born of fear instead of calm wisdom, a vicious cycle begins. The kingdom is lost and relationships with those around us become strained. We have slipped into the escalating cycle of fear, judgement, disempowerment then more fear. Soon we infect everyone in our environment and interactions go awry as whichever dysfunctional stance you take will provoke the opposite stance in them. If the wounded child is running your kingdom, and thus fear speaks out of your mouth, this will instantly provoke in your listener, their controlling advisors to respond. You shrink down fearfully, answering in the disempowered voice of a wounded child, which automatically provokes a finger wagging criticism your audience. This is how the cross communication of non-love between you and another human being occurs. In that moment, the kingdom is lost as you are no longer present to keep things steady and calm, and neither is that person with whom you are interacting. Instead, both kingdoms are being run by *peasants* and advisors.

Quinto and I like to demonstrate how communications can go awry in this way. We role play as, three times he asks me this simple question, "Have you seen my shoes?", to which I will respond each time in one of the following ways.

I.   I shrink down and whine, *"It's not my fault, how am I supposed to know where they are?"* Yes, I am coming from my wounded child.

II. I stand over him, pointing my finger accusingly saying, *"Well you should put your shoes in the right place shouldn't you?"*. Here I am coming from my inner critical parent. The advisors are speaking out of my mouth.

III. I calmly respond *"Yes, they're over there"* or *"No, I haven't"*. Now I am in my balanced, sovereign state which has no fear filled reaction.

As you can see, the first two reactions are from a kingdom out of balance. In examples *I* . and *II*. the sovereign is not in command and the reactions are dysfunctional. The third reaction, however, is not driven by fear, it is merely a statement of fact, a calm response with no agenda. You can see how the first two reactions are like waving a red flag to a bull. They're bound to provoke a dysfunctional response, and **the response we provoke will always be the opposite of the stance we have taken**.

For example, I have reacted from the child stance in response *I.*, so that will provoke a parental response from my partner. In response *II.* I have reacted from a finger-wagging parental stance which is bound to provoke the wounded child in my partner. In response *III.* I am not provoking, simply remaining in my neutral sovereignty and thus my partner will also remain in balance. Even if they don't, if I persist in remaining in my calm, non-reactive, sovereign status, they will also return to such a status.

Now you have this information, it is fun to step back and watch people communicate with each other, to see who is actually running their kingdom. You will find it fascinating to realise how dysfunctionally they are interacting and you will begin to perceive whether they are coming from their child or parental or balanced sovereign state. As you observe, it will become obvious how disagreements and un-loving, fear driven, dialogues get started. Most important of all is for you to pay attention to your own situation, how you are reacting and what is that provoking in other?. It is utterly fascinating and truly enlightening!

REGAINING YOUR KINGDOM

So how do you prevent this takeover, this collapse and chaos of a kingdom ruled by fear? What is **the key** to regaining your leadership of your own life and re-establishing a calm, balanced, wise and benevolent kingdom? Indeed, a calm, balanced and happy world? It is simple, once you master the following methods.

The techniques I am about to teach you may seem awkward at first, but it is more than worthwhile persevering, as to master these is LIFE CHANGING! What you're going to do is reverse the polarities. That is, reverse the old habit of ignoring the *peasants* and listening to the advisors (or ignoring your inner wounded child and listening to your inner critical parental voices). If you want your life back, if you want joy restored, if you want to live in harmony with all around you, if you want to reclaim your own innate power and walk daily in the essence of love that you truly are, then use the following techniques.

Part one, how to handle the advisors is simple, but Part two, how to keep fear at bay, will take a bit more effort on your part. Persevere, keep practicing, it is worth the effort because, like learning to ride a bike, once you have mastered this you will be flying along with the wind in your hair feeling the joy of power and freedom like never before.

PART ONE

DISMISS THE ADVISORS (your internalised critical parent voices).

It's time to remember that those advisors work for you, they're under YOUR command, so you have to put them in their place before they get above themselves and squash you. Where you've been listening to their eroding criticisms and shaming words, firmly switch them off! So whenever you hear the undermining whisper, or maybe shout, of self criticism in your head, imagine this voice is coming from an advisor, sneaking the criticism into your right ear. **With the back of your right hand, swat swiftly up by your right ear, saying firmly and clearly "dismissed!" or "silence!".**

Yes, you can do it, you are taking back command of your kingdom. After all, these are YOUR advisors, your employees, they are supposed to be doing YOUR bidding, not the other way around. Dismiss them in a commanding and authoritative voice (not a whisper!). You make it quite clear that you are having none of it! Thus you can send them away as soon as they start to prattle on, so the 'brainwashing' cannot take a hold.

How do you know if they are there? Simple. You will hear those inner voices of put-down thoughts such as, "You're useless, you are worthless, you are a failure, you did that wrong again didn't you?". Now, instead of absorbing and reacting to such criticisms you stand firm in your power and repossess command of your kingdom. You will not hear a word of it, you stop them in their tracks. With that firm flick from the back of your right hand you will send them away, dismiss them, and remain empowered.

PART TWO

REASSURE the PEASANT (your internalised wounded child).

Next, and here's where the real work begins, you must get out of the habit of pushing aside and trying to ignore that inner voice of fear or worry, but instead embrace it and pay deep attention to the wounded part of yourself which is really the one feeling it. It is time to break the cycle of TURNING AWAY, and learn the new way of TURNING TOWARDS your inner frightened peasant, giving them your full attention and support.

It is not always easy to begin with, especially if you're someone who is unaccustomed to listening to your own deep emotions. As adults, we have spent years and years blotting out that painful landscape, running away from and burying the hurts. Not going THERE. However, only by turning around and allowing yourself to go towards the emotion, to actually listen to your unheard wounded inner child, can you hope to regain equilibrium and peace.

The first step is to really focus on "What am I FEELING right now?". The second step is to recognise this feeling is not YOURS but is coming from a wounded child piece of yourself, back in the past when this injury happened. The third step is to talk to and reassure that little one. The method follows.

For some this comes easily, for others it takes time. However, the freedom and lightness you will feel from mastering this technique will take you to another realm. Yes, it may seem awkward to begin with, but the more you practice the quicker you will get deeply into it and a whole new world will open up for you, I promise. Then you'll be freed at last, to move in the direction you most want it to.

This technique has only six steps, but it requires your full attention and effort, especially if you have never before cleared away the weeds that have grown up between your current adult self and those poor lost wounded child pieces of you that linger in the past, hoping or perhaps having given up hope, for someone to come along and actually care enough to listen, gently reassure and lovingly hold them. You will gain calm balance and fearless momentum, ultimately feeling the thrill of riding to your own liberty, your own joy, your own power and success. More than all of this, your own essence of love will be restored, which changes your perspective on life and relationships with everyone and everything around you. You'll step back fully into your true, perfect, self. A wonderful, achievable goal.

THE TECHNIQUE

Step 1. Become a detective of your feelings.
Track your own emotions. What are you feeling right now, this minute? If that feeling is not love, it is the right moment to use this technique. Whenever you feel an emotion that is NOT LOVE, it is time to do the following.

Step 2. Stop what you are doing.
Stop whatever you are doing so you can give that non-love feeling your full attention. Put your hands on your solar plexus (just above your navel) where emotions are stored. Close your eyes to allow the feeling to come forward. Focus all your attention on that emotion deep within, asking yourself "What exactly is this I am feeling?". Stay with it for a moment, eyes closed, hands resting on your solar plexus, until you can give that emotion a one word name, such as anger, resentment, fear, loneliness, frustration, sorrow or regret.

With your hands still resting on your solar plexus, the place behind which that emotion dwells, cup your hands and gently scoop the emotion out. Now, stretching your arms straight out in front of you, place the little child who is feeling this emotion, to stand there. Now you have externalised the emotion, it is no longer within you, in fact it is not yours. It belongs to this little child standing right in front of you, who is feeling it and looking helpless.

Step 3. Observe the little one.

Eyes still closed, in your mind's eye observe the child standing there as a younger version of you. As if transported back in time, see how old this little one is. Notice that they look just as you did at that age and are wearing what you would have worn then. Perhaps there was even a nickname they were called by their family back then. Start to visualise this lost and helpless little one's circumstances. Are they are alone in their room, or in some other setting where they feel there is no one there for them? No one who could help or understand them. Then into the scene visualise yourself, a wise, mature benevolent being of Light, an angel perhaps, gliding up to this dear, sweet and innocent little child with kindness, tenderness and with open hearted love.

Step 4. Ask gently, "What is the matter little one?"

Now it is time to listen, really listen. With all your regal, caring wisdom and compassion, be the support they have longed for. This lost, innocent one has felt unheard and invisible for so long, they might find it hard at first to really believe someone loving is finally there for them. Wait for this sweet child to answer to your inquiry, be patient and kind, maybe coax and reassure them that you are on their side. Whatever the non love emotion is that they are feeling (which you originally detected in your own solar plexus), resentment, anger, bitterness or sorrow, at the base of it will always be fear. Let the little one tell you the story that led up to this feeling. The story of what happened to frighten them. It may be a story you already know, but sometimes your inner wounded child, once really listened to and supported, will reveal things from the past you hadn't even remembered. You may have had no idea that those events had occurred and caused your younger self so much trauma, yet they are vital for you as an adult to be aware of. As you listen with full attention to the little one, you will hear them telling you their story and, with your eyes still closed, you may even visualise the event unfolding. This brings understanding and tenderness towards the little one who felt so frightened and alone, until now. Now they have someone of their very own, who will champion them!

Step 5. Reassure and support that little one.
Now you rise up to your status as the all supportive, benevolent and unconditionally loving sovereign. When you have heard why this helpless and lonely little one is feeling so afraid, your heart fills with compassion and love for their plight. Reassure them that they are not bad or wrong. They are merely a child so they couldn't possibly be to blame. Tell them that you have come to collect them. Let them know that they are safe now and that any time they may need you in the future, you will stop whatever you are doing, to listen and take care of them. It's as if you have become their new and ideal mummy and daddy, unconditionally loving, tender and kind, always available to listen, to offer reassurance and to support. They may be surprised and certainly relieved that at last there is someone on their side, someone to relieve their anxiety, loneliness and isolation. At long last, they have YOU. Allow them enough time to show and tell you all they need to, and respond as a benevolently loving parent would to a child. Most essentially tell them. IT'S NOT YOUR FAULT.

Step 6. Then enfold them in your arms.
Open your arms wide, let them run to you, as you say YOU ARE SAFE NOW. You truly understand them. They've come home at last, no longer left alone and isolated in that dark place of fear and confusion. You, the wise mature and loving presence, are going to always be there for them from now on, you will be their champion and their comfort, always ready to listen whenever they need you. Give them a great big hug, let them cry with relief or nestle peacefully into your arms. Then gently place them back in your solar plexus, welcoming them home!

Notice how different the world looks now, and how differently you are able to handle whatever situation you are in. Without fear running the show, your kingdom has returned to power, to love driven balance and flow. Now you have this technique, practice it every day. Remember, like learning any new skill, the only way you can enjoy flying along feeling the exhilaration of freedom and balance, is to try and try, practice and practice, till you have mastered it.

The hardest part is remembering to track your emotions, constantly checking in with yourself during the day to see what you are feeling at any moment, but particularly when you feel uncomfortable. If you detect a feeling that is not love, the little one needs you. So STOP what you are doing, take the little one out, truly listen and reassure them, follow the technique to its conclusion. You have very many little ones to take care of ranging in age from pre-birth to late teens, and each of them has waited for you for a VERY, VERY LONG TIME. At first it is hard to remain alert to non-love emotions, to externalise them and give them your undivided attention, but with practice it will gradually become second nature. I have seen such wonderful and positive life changes in those who practice this method. Here is one example:

I had an astrology client who wanted me to do a compatibility study for herself and her fiancé. Their wedding day was drawing nearer and she feared she might be making a mistake and came to me seeking clarification before it was too late. After plotting and fully examining their charts side by side, happily I was able to see that they were indeed wonderfully matched as true partners, with the potential to enjoy a long and happy life together. So what was the problem?

She was downhearted because they kept arguing. They could not seem to stop, and she was ready to give up. So I taught her the above method and advised her that even when you are right in the middle of an argument, you can simply say, "Could you give me a minute please?" and go to a place where you can be alone and do the exercise of really listening to what is worrying your inner wounded child. I further explained that, once she had completed this and reassured the little one, she could go back to talking with her fiancé. "But how can I do that?", she protested, "We live in a small flat"?. Simple, just go to the bathroom. After all, you can talk to your wounded child anywhere that is private. Three weeks later she returned, beaming and with eyes sparkling. "It worked, we're not arguing any more!". Not only had she mastered the technique but she had also taught it to her fiancé, enabling them to both take personal responsibility for their own wounds instead of expecting the other one to fix them. I am delighted to report that, after all these years, they are still happily married, and remain in a joyful and balanced relationship by continuing to use this technique. Couples benefit tremendously from having this technique in their toolkit. It reminds them to take personal responsibility and not expect their partner to fix them. Nor to not take unbalanced reactions personally, instead to simply ask "who is here?" in a calm way. The partner can then realise that it was not their empowered self speaking out of their mouth, but their internalised fearful wounded child or critical parent. In fact, it is fascinating to observe that the one truly speaking to you when critical or undermining phrases are launched out, is actually that person's parents. No point in trying to dialogue with his or her parents, you will need to wait until the king is back on the throne before anything can be resolved!

The tragedy of living in fear causes so much ill in the world, yet people are unaware that deep down inside they are triggered by childhood wounds which they have never accessed and thus never addressed. Now that you know this, take a look around you. Observe how human beings are behaving and interacting in all situations every day. You will start to detect when a person is coming from:

a) fear - the frightened *peasant* is running the kingdom.
b) control - the undermining advisors are creating domineering behaviour.
c) love - the King/Queen is calm and balanced, fully empowered and loving.

By a lifetime of overriding our feelings, we programme ourselves to ignore the very things that we most need to pay attention to and deal with. It is amazing therefore how, once you begin listening to your solar plexus, to what emotion is actually being felt, you become so much brighter, happier and more balanced. By embracing and trying this technique you'll begin caring for that wounded child every single time they need you, which is the vital action that has been missing in your life. When you start tracing negative emotions back to where they sprouted and detach the wounded child from yourself, you will be free to **observe rather than be the drama.** By truly listening to what that lonely, isolated little boy or girl has been longing to say, you can draw on your balanced, empowered and wise adult self, to truly care for that helpless one who was so lost, so traumatised, in a way they have never been cared for before. Once you learn how and when the seed was sown, you can clear the weeds and overgrowth from your emotional garden and start to bathe in its beauty and Light again, taking that little one by the hand and enjoying every moment of every day with them, as they feel safe and cherished by you.

It all starts with you becoming a detective, to track your own emotions.

So REMEMBER – every moment of every day be alert to your feelings. If you detect a feeling welling up that is NOT LOVE, you know what you must do. Stop, externalise and care for the helpless little one. Remember, your wounded child comes first, before even your own children! By living life this way, by taking care of your own stuff (no-one else can do this as they did not experience things as you did when you were growing up), everyone will benefit, especially those closest to you. Ultimately, by healing yourself you are healing the world as, by changing your own dance steps for the better, everyone around you will adjust their steps for the better too.

Transactional Analysis concepts were originated by Eric Berne.

CHAPTER 8
Money and Manifesting

MONEY, WHAT IS IT AND HOW TO GET IT

What are YOU worth? Who is this YOU that is worth something or nothing? Do you fear money, or the lack of it? Do you carry a script from your parents that says money is a constant headache? Or, from the way you were brought up, do you feel that you are of little value? For far too many people money is a 'dirty' word. After all, aren't we taught it is the "root of all evil"? All the negative connotations centred around money are not truly about the inanimate paper notes or jingling coins. They are about the people who impress their energy, their fears, hopes and prejudices upon those items.

How about a whole new concept. Let's turn our human prejudice on its head and say.... Money is LOVE. Yes, you heard me right. Money is love. Knowing this can alter your inbuilt restrictions or superstitions about its magic and right there you start to open the gates to your own prosperity, rather than keeping them locked shut.

WHY MONEY CAN BE LOVE

Imagine you see a painting you really love. You use money to buy it. The person who painted that picture was doing what they love to do. So you are buying love, the love they put into their work, with your money. You have exchanged your money for the love energy imbued by the artist into the painting as they created it. Also you are feeling love as you immerse yourself in the painting and place it on your wall. The artist now has money and they hear a piece of music that lifts their heart, so they use the money you gave them in exchange for something they love too, that piece of music they love. The musician created that soundscape because they were doing what they love to do too, so their music is filled with their love. Thus,

111

in an ideal world, the money would be an exchange of love for love, all the way down the line.

This is why it is so important to be careful when you choose what to do with your energy. Working just to gain money for material things or worse still, to stockpile it and worship it for its own sake, will not be about an exchange of love and thus will not be putting the energy of love out into the universe. But working with love, doing the things you love to do, will automatically impregnate your creations with love. Then those who enjoy the fruits of your labour will be dealing in love. Be sure, therefore, to always follow your heart when it comes to how you earn. Be authentic, be sincere and most importantly of all, do what you truly love to do.

Money flows, rather like a river. It is pointless feeling shame or a sense of undeserving about receiving money, because it is never really yours is it? Any money you receive does not stay with you forever, unless you are a miser. It is simply passing through, taking a temporary stay at your doorstep before moving on to the next person and so on. How beautiful to see this as a constant flow of passing on the energy and the love. Unfortunately, the miserly and the greedy act like a dam in the river, collecting a lake for themselves while those further down the line become parched and dry, and inevitably have less and less available to pass on to the next person to maintain the flow. Greed causes energetic dehydration, which leads to a loveless dry desert.

If you allow your job to generate in you the energy of resentment, restriction, sacrifice or compromise, you are blocking the flow of love in the universe. This is why Quinto and I tell those who come for therapy and healing, "Do what you LOVE to do, rather than doing something just for the money". If you go deep within and allow yourself to feel what your heart would love to do, what it deeply desires to create, you will know in which direction to put your energy and will be focussed on what you genuinely desire. Do not restrict yourself by creating self-sabotaging games with inner voices of fear and scarcity. When we love what we create, we will do it so well that everybody will want a piece of it. Thus, as I wrote in Chapter 5, about love, it becomes an exchange of energy with no effort.

It can be very hard for some people to truly hear the voice within that tells them what is their passion, what they would dearly love to do, and even harder to trust that it will be financially sustaining. Yet that is exactly how the universe works. Before you incarnated you chose to share your gifts with humanity. Indeed you made a soul contract to do so. Surely then, to hold back and undervalue these gifts by taking on a job you do not enjoy, compromising because you fear being left high and dry, is to break the contract you made when you gained a place at this University for the Soul called Earth.

It is vital, therefore, to listen to your deepest voice, listen to your gut, to remember what you truly love to do. If necessary, go back to childhood and remember what you most loved to spend your time doing. Unfortunately we live in a society that leads us to believe we don't have a right to spend our energy doing what we most feel drawn to do, we don't have the time and won't have the necessary status if we simply follow our dreams. So we start to toe the line, suppressing our true nature to achieve 'success' in the eyes of a boss, a parents, neighbours or peers, and to stave off the fear of being left with nothing (of not getting our milk!).

Part of the healing of this misconception is to track back and observe your childhood, remembering the attitude towards money in your environment, and from the authority figures who influenced you, your parent, teacher or priest. It is vitally important to track your own limiting and self-sabotaging beliefs and look deeply into how they came about in the first place, because **beliefs are the filters of reality**. If you believe you cannot do the work you would love to do because it doesn't pay enough, if you believe you need a bigger and better house, style, wardrobe, vehicle, think again. Do not be bamboozled by the messages from the commercial world, telling you that in order to be an OK human being you need to own more and more, and thus have to keep up by earning more and more. Instead of fearing the judgement of the outside world, or fearing being left out and left behind, go within, get back in touch with and honour who you truly are. Yes, re-kindle your dreams and follow them with absolute trust. Because doing what you truly love to do WILL generate an income.

Humans are by nature creative creatures. So become aware of where you are focussing your attention. If it is on doom and gloom, that is what you will create. If it is on contentment and fulfilment rather than extreme wealth, then that is what you will create. And you will create it by being quite naturally and instinctively creative!

More and more people come to us for guidance nowadays with the wish to find their way back onto their true path. We hear over and over the question "**What is my true purpose?**". They feel they have lost touch with their own inner guidance. It has somehow been overruled, glossed over, stamped out of them, by authorities and false knowledge.

It is part of the flow of this current Aquarian age, an era in which we human beings are less and less willing to compromise our time and energy, that we are increasingly drawn to finding our deeper authentic self and seeking the fulfilment of our individual harmonic destiny. We are sensing that we have wishes and passions simply waiting to blossom that have been suppressed for so long that they are hard to find, hard to resurrect. So if you are one of those, remember that you are supremely creative and powerful and that it is more than your desire, it is your DUTY to share your natural gifts with humanity. By doing so, instead of chasing the money, the money will start to chase you! All it takes is a big leap of faith to re-start the flow.

To attract just what you need, in all senses including material and financial, it is vital that you step into TRUST. The only limitations are the ones you impose on yourself. Once you have tracked down where you learned those limitations, you can dismiss them. Then you will be on your way to the secure knowledge that all your needs will always be met. Ironically, it is when you trust this to be so, that the universe naturally brings to your door exactly what you need.

If you are not sure what it is that you really want to do, you have lost touch with a vital part of yourself. So set aside the time to start the detective work. Again, going backwards is the only way to go forwards. So go inside, remember what you loved to do, what your dreams and goals were when you were young, before duty and adaptation took over. Allow memories from your childhood to filter up until you reach that "Aha!" moment, which will give you the key to your true goals. Do you realise what has got in the way of your deep self-fulfilment, what has put a wall across the path to your true purpose? Fear, and it all goes right back to that initial, primal fear, fear of failing on your mission and of course ultimately **fear of not getting your milk** and therefore dying. When you start to master the techniques laid out in Chapter 7, you can take your inner wounded child by the hand and together enjoy the things he or she longed to do, right now in your life.

YOUR AUTHENTIC SELF DESERVES THE BEST

No-one can be authentic unless they deeply connect with themselves. As a coping mechanism we put up barriers. We feel uncomfortable, discordant in our surroundings, out of focus with the world. How can we be the God or Goddess that we truly are, how can we be of any help to humanity and the planet unless we go and see, feel and fulfil the core of our own needs? When we lived as tribal people in nature and from nature, we knew justice and balance, but in the modern world all that has become detached and far from us. We have lost our connection to what is real and thus, to our deepest self. Modern society introduced the concept of work for money, but is this kind of work a true expression of your creativity or is it just a duty to get the cash in?

Ask yourself the following questions to start you on the journey towards all round wealth. Wealth of body, mind and soul. Where were you and in what environment when you last felt true inner peace and happiness? Do you believe that is not a reality you can live every day? Do you see life as a sacrifice in which you sell your soul just to get some money? Do you work in order to be recognised or applauded for material status expressed by your possessions that show the world you are worth something as a person? Are you constantly bombarded by advertising that tells you all the things you are lacking but must have in order to be good enough, to be accepted, to be safe, to be loved? Do you feel overwhelmed by the persuasive voices which distract you from what is real and true and sincere in your heart?

Or, do you sense that you do indeed make the most of your precious chance in this life to express your personal gifts, sharing your true essence with humanity? Do you live as your authentic self, spending each day doing what you love to do in an environment that matches your soul? Do you see life as an opportunity to celebrate, enjoy and share your uniqueness, your gifts and your beauty with the world, certain that all your needs will be fulfilled as the universe lives in sublime balance?

Which of these two lives would you prefer to be living? We have been lead down a path that has taken us far from what is real. We are hounded by the publicity and persuaders that demand our attention and life force, convincing us that we have to stay on the treadmill of sacrifice to get the material toys that will bring happiness, fulfilment and acceptance.

Only when we are stripped back to basics, through loss or when on vacation camping in nature, do we reconnect with what is real. Close your eyes and imagine for a moment, yourself standing on a path with absolutely nothing, no belongings, no money, no home. Or if, like so many including myself, you have at some stage in your life genuinely lost absolutely everything and been stripped back to basics. In that moment you will remember the essential truth, that you genuinely only need, FIVE things. Food, water, shelter, health and love. I would also add a sixth, time, but when you have the first five, time will always be yours. So anything beyond those magic five essentials is actually the icing on the cake. How interesting it is to play with this concept. Good food, good water, shelter, time to have the freedom to be in contact with your deepest self and your unique gifts, and to share them with others with love. Funnily enough, good health will also naturally follow if you have all of those things.

As human history has progressed, all of these things have been taken from us or contaminated. Food is processed, as is water and time is sold to the highest bidder. Is it possible that the money we get for our slavery puts us into the hands of the corporations, whose gain is from our loss, as they convince us into another slavery – materialism? Ownership of land and property is a strange concept to native peoples, who know it is not a reality, as the only thing you can take with you when you die is your soul. Even your body must be left behind. So true wealth is within the soul, wealth of inner connection and personal fulfilment from which springs kindness, understanding, generosity, compassion, gratitude and appreciation for all that is around us. We feel this most when bathed in the glories of nature. We feel humbled and grateful for so much that is given daily for our survival and pleasure, by the elements of which we are comprised; the waters, the sun, the plants and trees and our blessed Mother Earth. Who does not sigh with pleasure and feel fully connected when gazing at the stars, observing a beautiful sunset or following the magic of a rainbow. That is true wealth.

If money is love, and love is blotted out by fear, then money and fear are never able to live together healthily. As you chase the next dollar, it is good to remember that the money you seek is never yours, it is merely passing through you to the next person, you are a mere conduit. Once you cease to fear it's concept, money will continuously flow into and through your life, with limitless abundance, as a flowing river of love.

HOW TO MANIFEST

To some, manifesting seems like an elusive magic trick. Surely I, a simple human, do not have the power or right to change the world for my own benefit? My mother certainly believed that, yet as a teenager I began to play with the concept of visualising something into reality. Then one day as my mother was frustratedly driving around looking for a parking space I decided to visualise someone vacating a space just around the next corner. I told her "There will be one just around this corner". As the driver was reversing out of the space I told her what I had done. She immediately fell into her shame conditioning. "How could you do such a thing? He might have needed that space".

As mentioned, we humans have a long history of shame and undeserving to overcome. This is taught to us from very young. As a result, the accusing finger wagging in our brain blocks our belief in our right to receive whatever we truly want. Remember the phrase *"Be careful what you wish for"*? It sounds like a warning against seeking your heart's desire, as if that were so wrong that you'd be punished in some way for daring to go there. Even worse might happen if you actually *asked* for what you want. Thus we fear going after the very things we most desire and have lost belief in our innate ability and right, to manifest them for ourselves.

As you now know, fear is the diametric opposite to love. Fear, through indoctrination by religion and superstition, takes us far from remembering how innately powerful we are to create and be whatever we truly wish for. When I manifested that parking space it was with the clear belief I could achieve it, before being shamed by my mother for being 'selfish'. If only I had realised then what I know now. That when we manifest our heart's desire it is within the synchronicity of the universe. It causes no harm, because that driver in that moment needed to drive away for his own reasons, just as we needed that parking space. All was, and is, in a perfect dance of harmony.

We cannot manifest through synchronicity and accord if we are drowning in fear. However if we live in, and are **motivated by, love**, then we naturally and smoothly manifest whatever we wish for, as it is automatically in harmony with the universe. It is in that state of grace and love, that you can live in the natural flow of life, staying tuned in to your external environment and your intuition. Your desires then are neither risky nor dangerous, and will never harm anyone, in fact they will contribute to the flow of nature and the cosmos.

So let us take another look at that phrase *"Be careful what you wish for"*. Instead of a warning, let us see it as a reminder to you to take care over the details of your request when making it. The phrase, instead of a warning, can be seen as a confirmation that you are supremely powerful and **can** manifest whatever you wish for. That phrase does not signify you don't deserve to have your heart's desire. It does not mean that by having what you want you'll somehow be hurting or depriving someone else, nor does it mean that you had better be careful or you will be punished for having dared to wish for something for yourself! Instead, try interpreting its meaning as 'Be careful over the details before you send your wish out to the universe for fulfilment'. With that slant on the warning, it confirms that you CAN manifest what you ask for, you just have to be careful about the clarity of your request. So it makes sense that you are being warned to do the groundwork and become very clear about what you actually want, all the details and parameters, before 'sending in your order'.

Many years ago I needed a car for my work teaching Shamanism. I thought it through very carefully. I needed something that could go off road, with the capacity to carry all the paraphernalia of drums, blankets, etc. I had a few other details that I fine-tuned and having done my research it came down to only one make and model that would fit all the criteria. Now there were two obstacles, but I had absolute faith these could be overcome. The first obstacle was that I didn't actually have the money to afford such a vehicle, and the second obstacle was that an off-road vehicle or 4x4 would be harmful to the environment, which I was averse to. So into my request, my magical manifesting spell, I added "And not harmful to the environment". Within days I saw an advert in the local newspaper for the very vehicle I knew I needed. Strangely, it was for sale in the very town where my friend mentioned he was headed to the next morning. So I asked him to check out the car for me, which he did. Then he phoned and told me the car seemed in good shape, but the strange thing was that it had been converted to run on LPG gas, which is much less harmful to the environment. I was delighted and said "That's my car"! I had no doubts as I made my appointment with the bank, that they would lend me the money even though they had no reason to. And they did.

So you can have your wishes fulfilled, your prayers answered, as long as you are clear about every detail. Don't worry about barriers such as "How will I afford it?" or "I have nowhere to park it". Simply specify that you need those details taken care of too. Then be practical and help your angels to manifest your wishes. Money will be no object as you can manifest that too. Again, arm yourself with information, do the research to find out how you can possibly gain the money to pay for your wish. And it will be granted.

Here is an exercise I often do with my students. Pick out a speck on the floor in front of you. Now imagine that you are an all-powerful angel looking down on that speck, which is the human in your care. Your little human is in need of something. Imagine they have just looked up to the heavens and said "I need a car". How do you feel, as their angel who can bring them their heart's desire? You need more information of course, don't you? What kind of car, what colour, what's the main purpose, etc. So the more clear your little human can be, the more accurately you, as their angel, can fulfil their wish without confusion or error. But a vague request from them would leave you wondering what exactly DO they want and you might end up unable to proceed with its fulfilment until you received further clarification.

So now you know. Being *careful what you wish for* means firstly that you must take great care to call in **exactly** what you do need and secondly you must take care to recognise the consequences of your desire being fulfilled, from something as simple as a parking space for your car, to something more complicated like a car itself. If you have been really clear with the details you can be CERTAIN your wish will be granted.

Manifesting is rather like ordering something online. You start with an idea of something you need or want, you select the exact make, model and colour, also being specific about any details that are important to you. Then you send your order off, trusting that it will be fulfilled. So to be sure you to get the very thing you want, be very clear about all the specifics, then simply place your order giving as much detail as possible. Now relax and know without a shred of doubt that it is on its way. When you are motivated by love instead of greed, there's no need to think about it until it arrives. It might arrive in one delivery, for example that specific car, or it might come in several smaller packages, if, for example, you have requested a certain sum of money.

As with ordering on line, once you've put your order in, you don't spend every day wondering if it will really happen or whether you deserve it, or feel ashamed for having had the audacity to ask for this, do you? You simply and with complete faith, await its arrival. Unless, that is, you are a particularly un-trusting and anxious type, in which case, because you are a supremely powerful being, you just might manifest the disappointment you seek.

In all cases and with all orders, these are the essential steps.

i) TRUST
    -   in yourself, in your own power and the right to manifest,
    -   that the outcome will be to the highest possible good for all,
    -   that your request will be heard by the universe and will be fulfilled.

ii) DECIDE
    -   Be unafraid to go for that which you most need.
    -   Allow yourself to follow your heart's desire. Only by letting go of fear and prejudice will you be able to hear your inner intuitive voice, in order to attain this.
    -   You are about to place an order. Do the research, KNOW what you want.

iii) BE SPECIFIC
    -   Your own team of helpers (call them angels, guides, the universe, Great Spirit or your higher self, whatever feels right) are standing by, waiting to fulfil your request.

- For that reason you must be very specific about what you want, with as much detail as you can, including why you want this.
- Any vagueness will lead to failure.

iv) PLACE YOUR ORDER
- This can be done just by visualising it clearly with INTENTION,
- or in prayer as a specific request, holding a clear picture in your mind
- or by the ritual of writing it down on a piece of paper, even drawing it then putting the paper away or burying it (not going back and checking it over and over as that would be the opposite of trust).
- you can pay for your order with a gratitude ceremony or by the sharing of your innate gifts with humanity.

v) LET IT GO WITH COMPLETE CONFIDENCE
- Trust that, from the moment you've placed your order, the universe is working to deliver it to you.
- There is nothing further for your conscious mind to do, so don't think about it.
- **Know, without doubt**, that it is on its way, let go.

vi) BE GRATEFUL
- Recognise, with gratitude, that the universe has heard your voice and is fulfilling your request.
- When it is obvious that your order is being fulfilled, either bit by bit or all at once, say thank you to your helpers (personal guides, angels, Great Spirit).
- There is no price to pay, but in gratitude you might want to make a kindly gesture to someone else to keep the good vibes and energetic balance flowing.

vii) BE AWARE
- You deserve what you ask for.
- We are all instruments of the fulfilment of others' dreams as well as our own.
- The universe is in a magical dance of harmony, all is well.

As essentially creative beings, we humans have the capacity and gifts to design, make and fix things, we are even able to create new life from our own bodies. We are truly astonishing creatures as whatever we focus our attention on we create. **Attention = intention = creation.** You are a born manifestor. Not only have you been manifesting all through your life, but remember, you have also manifested and styled YOUR LIFE before you even arrived here. You had the power to design your personal life movie, plus all the lessons and gifts that would be uniquely yours, to grow the parts of yourself that needed growing. Thus you are supremely powerful. You are not simply the created, you are also the creator, an expression of God, and thus YOU CAN CREATE whatever you wish to manifest. There are truly no limits.

We are trained to forget this fact when we incarnate, and that forgetting does have its purpose. The purpose being that we might live each day as an experience, surprised and challenged enough to draw on our deepest inner strengths in order to learn the lessons that will make us great, wise and illuminated. We struggle, pushing the rock uphill without remembering that we can simply move it up there through intention if we call on our own will and our unseen helpers!

It is by remembering this power and ability to manifest that you can tap into whichever channel in the universe you desire, your spiritual or celestial shopping channel, and place an order for whatever it is you need for the fulfilment of your journey and your mission. Modern scientists, working in the nano field, have proven that everything is connected, thus there are no barriers between you and what you choose to receive, so just reach out and draw it to you.

ITS OK

Its OK to receive. There is not a dastardly or evil price to pay. The universe will provide exactly the right balance and will bring to you what you have requested. The method by which your request can be fulfilled will become clear to you. For example, if it is a specific sum of money you've asked for, you will very quickly be given the opportunities to earn or fundraise that amount. Everything in the universe works in balance. You receive and you give. And you give within the realms of your own abilities, gifts and skills. Payment for your order will not come in the form of punishment, but will come in the call to use and share your innate gifts and skills.

The universe is in an eternal and extraordinarily beautiful dance of balance. When we give too much we become depleted, when we take too much we become engorged. Remaining in balance is to remain healthy in mind, body and spirit.

Many years ago, when I first started sharing my healing and psychic gifts I resisted charging for my services, feeling I should just give them away. But a wise elder who had worked for many years also as a healer, pointed out a fundamental and profound truth. Everything works in balance, and thus when we give our gifts and skills, whether as an artist, a healer or an accountant, there is an automatic exchange of energy taking place. Thus, the wise elder explained that if I did not charge for my services I would be walking away with a piece of my client's soul, as exchange would always automatically take place. I was horrified. I did not want to own a piece of anybody! Having grown up so restricted and controlled, I was hyper-conscious and respectful of each individual and animal's freedom, so the thought of owning any part of another being was abhorrent to me. From that moment I took on the vital truth that it is not only OK, it is actually **essential** to request a fair exchange for what is given. You can do this too, with no shame. Equally it is important to remember, if you take something without paying a fair price for it, a piece of you will be taken energetically in exchange, in which case, instead of gaining at the expense of another you will ultimately lose. That is the balance of the universe. You came to Earth in possession of strengths and skills that the planet and its beings could make use of and value. In exchange for the sharing of these innate gifts of yours, you can have whatever you wish for. All you have to do is ask.

Education has a price too. When you chose to come back to spend time again at this university for the soul known as Earth, you were asked how you might pay for your course. The answer to this question came from deep within your soul "I have these specific gifts to share with humanity". Thus the agreement was made and balance established. If you fail to share your truly innate gifts, you are breaking the contract! Of course, still remember that sharing your gifts with humanity must be valued by those who receive their benefit, and thus the chain of exchanges can flow on. A fair price too, because, if the recipient does not value the personal gifts and energy you have shared, they may waste them.

So it is by listening to your heart's desire and allowing yourself to become immersed in the energy of your natural gifts, then sharing them and asking a fair price, you are not being selfish or greedy, quite the opposite. You are sending out into the world what the world needs and which you agreed long ago to share from your deepest self! Whether the gift is as an artist, a healer, a mathematician or a manager, if these seeds are to be cared for after they are sewn, they must be treasured by the recipient.

It is not just money or things that you can manifest. You are so powerful that you can also heal yourself and invoke healing in others, if it is their wish. After all, healing is also about putting in a request then trusting implicitly that the wish will be granted. Again, when you make that order to the online shop, you know the product will arrive because you have paid the required fee. So what might that fee be?

On a daily basis we receive from the elements and all of nature, often without paying for it. The ancient peoples lived so close to, and dependent upon, nature that their philosophies and rituals were based on observing the constant energetic exchanges that were taking place in every way and every where. Their payments were powerful as their full attention, spirit and energy would be given to performing sacred rituals. In the western world we have lost the art of expressing our gratitude and wishing to restore balance, through ritual. Why not remind yourself how? It might be in the form of a prayer, the lighting of a candle, the setting up of a prayer altar or your gift to the spirits could be a dance or a song. You will automatically sense what feels right and fair.

BE CONTENT

There will be times in your life when you genuinely need something. You can manifest what you need, yet there is another side to this coin which is a part of the beauty of manifesting. As important as it is to recognise your power to manifest your heart's desire, it is equally important for you to tune in to appreciation and contentment with what you already have. Let your heart be warmed by valuing every thing and every one within your personal environment. Without allowing any of the old scripts of undeservedness or the new commercial brainwashings of need, to overshadow this consciousness of wealth.

Be truly aware of your blessings and sit with them simply bathed in the joy of being alive. Become conscious of how fortunate you are, how much the universe is supporting you, value your daily sustainment. Gratitude is a powerful energy exchange. People used to say grace before eating a meal, this was a form of exchange. Ancient peoples did rituals of gratitude and honour, in order to sustain their supply of food and water. When we honour the Creator we remember that we, too, carry the Creator within us.

Every cell in your body is made from what is created by and for you. The gifts of the universe are constantly on offer for your survival. Look around you, see the beauty that is given to you every day, from the air you breathe, the glorious clouds, grandfather sun or grandmother moon lighting your way and Mother Earth eternally producing and offering everything required for food and shelter. It is so hard to do this when you are shut in boxes, cars, offices, artificially heated homes, in your daily life.

So it is vital to your soul and connections and vital to the success of manifesting, for you to see and value the exchanges of love that permeate your life, by spending sacred time in the natural world. Just as the plants and trees love to receive the carbon dioxide you exhale as much as you love to receive the oxygen they exhale, so it is with manifesting. Where love replaces fear there is balance and flow, an effortless and natural exchange of energy. All your needs will be met, and it is always OK to ask.

CHAPTER 9
Health

BODY HEALTH

"Your body is a magnificent self-healing, self-repairing system and an organic wonder that you have yet to truly appreciate" Barbara Marciniak

The greatest possession you will ever own is your body. Take good care of it, do not fill it with the wrong fuel. Do not run from it, but run towards it. Such things that take you into deeper relationship with your body are yoga, pilates, sports, sex, dance and meditation. Some things that take you far from your own body are junk food, drugs, alcohol and workaholism.

In our modern human world we have developed the myth that our body is a separate and mysterious entity that could let us down or attack us at any moment. Patients who have experienced a 'heart attack' live in fear that their heart may 'attack' them again, as if it were an enemy. When we are damaged or sick we can be fearful of or become annoyed with our body, seeing it as working against us. Yet nothing could be further from the truth.

Every cell of your body is working FOR YOU, doing its utmost to maintain for you a healthy vessel. Day in and day out your cells labour endlessly on your behalf. Yet all too often you either take those loyal and dutiful servants for granted, ignore them, abuse them or even fear them, forgetting entirely that you are the captain of your physical ship and that they look, and answer, to you for direction.

Imagine for a moment that the cells of your body are your loyal subjects who long for their regent's attention, for your appreciation, your acknowledgement and your support. Rather like the teaching in Chapter 7, where you learned that to be emotionally healthy you need to stop turning away from but instead turn **towards** your wounded inner child as an empowered sovereign, so it is with the cells of your body. Instead of resisting their call for help and attention and thinking of them in the very least as an irritation and at worst as an enemy, the cells of your body need you, the master, to pay them appreciative and wise attention. Throughout history you can see examples of what happens when the ruler loses touch with the needs of his subjects. Chaos ensues. So it is vital for you to take on this empowered role of captain and leader, in order to guide and help your loyal cells.

The most profound way to do this is through deep meditation, going within your body. But for a quick pain fix, pay attention to the sensation of pain. Rather than running from it, go with your consciousness towards it, analyse it with "What is this sensation called pain?" and miraculously it may well stop. That is because you will have closed the pain gates that send messages to your brain. Once you have connected to the location of the pain's source, thank the cells there for alerting you to a problem, then tell them they are off duty now as you are 'onto it', you'll take it from here. It will seem strange at first because we have from our earliest years, been given the brainwashing that we are not in control and we have never certainly never been encouraged to talk with our body's cells.

We race through life, always meaning to be more diligent in our exercise or diet regimes, but we don't have enough time or energy or motivation, do we? These excuses are self-sabotaging, as you know how wonderful it feels when you overcome inertia and take yourself out for a wonderful walk, go to the gym or for a swim. When you take an exercise or yoga class you experience the magic of going within and re-connecting with your own vehicle. It feels so good to develop a great relationship with your own body, doesn't it?

In our healing work, Quinto and I bring people back to their own body and cell awareness, to facilitate re-balancing on a deep level. Some of the methods we may use to achieve this deep reconnection are shamanic drumming, sounds and chanting, energy realignment and journeying. From tailored personal meditations to sound baths for very large groups, each participant will go on their own personal journey within. During such group healing performances we have no plan for the soundscape that will be created, we simply step aside in trust to allow the healing vibration, music and words to come through. Much the same as we would do when downloading messages. We receive beautiful comments and gratitude from those who experience this inner reconnection and revelation, but we are simply the catalyst. The magic is not held within us nor in our performance, we are just facilitators as it is you, the participants, who are achieving the result.

Here is a beautiful message, right now, for you from Quinto

"I was feeling to tell you how strictly connected with the two powers of ATTENTION and INTENTION is TIME. How much of your time do you dedicate to honouring your inner self, to do what you LOVE to do, to being connected to your true self, to respecting your own feelings and your own precious time. How much are you forced during the day to do what is not yours, how much are you putting yourself every day in the condition that does not allow you to respect your true self and to live in the moment just doing things that satisfy you, spending time in a space of beauty and feeding your intention.

If you give attention to ugliness and disaster, to horrible news that is being projected towards you every day, that is a waste of your attention. You are spending your precious time giving power away to those who will tell you there is something wrong, something bad has happened or that life is violent and dangerous, then of course you are going to resonate with those things. The wonderful machine that is your body, it resonates with and adapts to every instant of the day, constantly. If you think about what is happening to your internal organs, your body is a perfect transformational machine, because it transforms everything you eat into something that is good for you, something that keeps you alive. All the oxygen is transformed in your cells because inside you is a micro-world in which every single organ does its job beautifully. And it happens without you even being aware of it, this job of transformation. There is a constant adapting to the air you breathe, the food and liquid you take into your body. Think about what you are feeding the cells to allow your beautifully designed system to work at its best.

In that transformational environment within which you live, you can use your time. Every day you have to dedicate enough time to create the universe and the reality that you want to create. Time to allow to unfold the manifestation of the energy within, the gifts you are born with and the beauty of connection. So stay focussed on the things that you love and spend time to give your attention every day to your body, to your SELF, your innate gifts and everything that allows you to become a better you, the best YOU that you know."

GROWTH IS A SPIRAL OF ENERGY

LIFE and its power are driven forward by the push of opposite energies. This push in two directions, positive and negative or masculine and feminine, creates momentum from which all growth occurs. Imagine a bird's eye view of two mules on opposite sides of a threshing circle, harnessed and joined to the centre. They start to move forward and though they are walking in opposite directions, this creates a circle and momentum. If both mules faced the same direction there would be no spin, no movement, no energy. By facing the opposite direction to its partner across the circle, each mule is contributing to the momentum. The spiral way in which plants and shells, flowers and even humans grow can be seen through the magnified patterns within them. They are ever increasing circles, driven by opposite poles of energy. It is even how we develop in the womb and the double-helix of our DNA is yet another spiral. The Fibonacci sequence is present in all life, it is the energy of opposites creating growth.

Within each of our billions of cells, this spin of energy is continuously turning, as our cells grow, blossom, serve, decrease, die, renew, regenerate and keep the cycle of our body's momentum and repair turning. In general, cancer is a situation where that normal spin goes out of control. Where, through inner and outer pollution, we corrupt that natural rhythm of spinning and growth, of essential decay and regeneration. When we wish to heal ourselves we must go within our own body and get into relationship with our cells, taking back our leadership role to return them into proper and healthy spin, but how does this become corrupted in the first place?

From the moment when the sperm of your father fused with the ovum of your mother, a miracle happened. Each cell knew its job as they were able to divide and form the pieces of you that were exactly right. The cells received instructions from your DNA, this one would become an ear, that one would become your toe, another one would divide and multiply to form your arm. And all along your spirit was the master of this phenomenal organisation. Each cell of your body knew who it was, what it's gifts were and how to behave to create and maintain the harmony of the whole. Yet in sickness those instructions have become interrupted and skewed. How does this happen? Simply this. They forget who they were meant to be and how they were instructed to perform. Does that sound familiar? Yes, it starts with your soul and your consciousness. Could the ultimate cause of day to day ill health and imbalance be that we forget WHO WE TRULY ARE. Because we are divorced from our true, perfect and original SELF by life experiences, by trauma, by family, by circumstances, by individuals, by groups, by influences, by contaminants. We are distracted, hypnotised, shocked, pulled out and taken further and further from our original divine essence.

We must hold in great esteem and have the utmost respect for those who chose to go through a major health challenge prior to incarnation. The person born with a disability or congenital abnormality that has no chance of a cure, is an especially old soul who has reached such a high level of development that their soul was capable of taking on such a mammoth task of suffering and learning in this lifetime. Remember, as explained at the beginning of this book, when we plan our forthcoming incarnation we are not permitted to take on more than we are capable of handling. Thus we can honour and respect such souls, as we do all souls in greatest suffering, as they are surely much further along the path towards unconditional love, than we are.

The ultimate healing tool is love but to find that within yourself you must go back to who you truly were before incarnating, back to the truth of and essence of YOU. When you remember, all your cells will remember too. When you recall that YOU are the master of your cells, they will respond in whatever manner you command them to, but mostly they will be reminded who they were truly meant to be when the programming originated and was perfect, then they can readjust themselves back to full and glorious healthy function.

In Chapter 6, I taught you the Daily Alignment, the first part of which you re-connected with the Light of unconditional love. By practicing that meditation daily you will begin to find it easy to draw on that golden-white healing Light. Then you can take it with you when you need to journey into your own body to perform repair and healing. Your body is stunningly beautiful on the inside. It is not a distant, dark and mysterious world, but a world of lights and vibrant colours. An exquisite and extraordinary landscape. The cells operate, receive instructions and send messages through light. All within your body is extraordinarily magical, so it is time go back, go take a visit, grow acquainted with this magnificent inner landscape. This is the way you can really get to know and develop a benevolent, enamoured and empowered relationship with your sacred vehicle.

THE ANCIENT WISDOM-KEEPERS KNEW

I have been blessed by so many people, ancient and modern, who have shared their wisdom over the years . One of these was a Mayan priest, whom I had invited as guest speaker to my conference on the magic and healing properties of the Crystal Skulls. Standing majestically before us in his full costume, about to reveal sacred and ancient secrets about life and the the phenomenally accurate Mayan calendar, he had us all on the edge of our seats. As I sat awaiting these profound revelations, with huge respect for this wise man, I was mystified by the first words that came out of his mouth. He simply said, as if everyone knew exactly what he was talking about, "Everything begins with the one and the zero". It was an enigmatic start to a talk explaining the Mayan cosmogony, and I sat there bemused, not knowing what on earth he had meant by the one and the zero. It seemed this great wise one was talking in riddles, so of course I was desperate to know the meaning of his profound yet obscure statement. I have often found that information coming from wisdom-keepers, whether in person or in spirit, comes through in riddles, which must be unravelled. As the talk went on, so much of the information shared was clear and wonderful, but it seemed this statement about the one and the zero was highly significant.

Later, from time to time, the phrase would pass through my mind and I would ponder on it's hidden meaning. Of course I had heard that computer coding is all about ones and zeros. Perhaps what he had meant was that the coding for all of life was about ones and zeros? Over time, the clues flitted across my radar and *everything begins with the one and the zero*' started to make sense. The 1 being a pole and the 0 being the circle through which it enters is of course a metaphor for the act of procreation. It also made total sense to me when looking at the ancient shamanic traditional medicine wheel. This circle, drawn on the ground with the cross connecting the four cardinal points has a pole at its centre, magically connecting the above with the below and all around it, the everything. And this symbology can also be seen as a zero with a one passing through it. The flat or horizontal wheel honours the energy lines running across Mother Earth (divine feminine) while the pole through the centre stands perpendicular, joining the Cosmos above (divine masculine) with her, making the fertile one and zero unification. The one being the stick and the zero being the circle spinning around it, the two opposite energies, the plus and the minus, the sacred and beautiful spin of life. So it is also with the ancient Native American sacred pipe ceremony. The pipe and the bowl are kept wrapped separately. Only when sacred ceremony begins are the two joined, the stone bowl representing the divine feminine or Mother Earth and the stem of the pipe representing the divine masculine or Father Sky. The symbol of the cross was always used in ancient times to represent Mother Earth, the horizontal line, united with Father Sky, the vertical line. Similarly the skull and the spine can be seen as a one and a zero. There are examples everywhere of the joining of these two opposites, the one and the zero, to trigger or signify creation.

By looking around me I began to realise that the one and the zero were everywhere, as the two energies that represent life. If you were to look at the one and the zero of a medicine wheel from above it might resemble a bull's eye. From the very beginning of our life on Earth we are stimulated by this one and zero target symbol. We start life drawn to the circle of our mother's breast and the target (nipple) from which all sustenance will come and through which our very survival is dependent. We live as people connecting with others through looking into their eyes, each another circle with a dot in it. We recognise on the deepest of levels, this symbol of the spin of all life, also represented by every cell and it's nucleus, within our bodies.

AN OUT OF BALANCE BODY IS A SICK BODY

Long before major illness starts we get the warning signs that things are not right, that we are out of balance. We each carry divine masculine and divine feminine energy within our cells. When this is in balance they do their job harmoniously and will keep us healthy, but if the balance between our personal inner masculine and feminine goes out, we give our cells no option but to follow our lead and also go out of balance. Too much of one or the other energy throws the switch, eventually the cells either over-produce, which may lead to a tumour, or under-produce, which may lead to an ulcer or breaking down of tissue.

Illness does not happen overnight. We sense imbalance in our lives long before our body finally starts to malfunction. Yet we silence that inner voice guiding us to take better care of our vehicle, telling us it is time to stop and rest and that we do not need to push ourselves into a performance or into being a super-hero. The inner wisdom that warns us we are not being kind by putting poison into our body, or that tells us we have an emotional issue that needs our loving attention, is overruled, so we are betraying the very body that serves us so faithfully. Thus, instead of living our authentic life following our natural intuition, we ignore the signs and our own needs, which is a form of abuse to our own cells, so sooner or later they break down. Why do we do this? Because we have allowed fear to rule our kingdom. Ironically, as stated earlier, the ultimate fear is that we are going to die, yet this fear can drive us to run away from the very thing that will keep us alive, listening to our body's needs and respecting them. Going back to the beginning, to our real essence and remembering who we truly are will put us back in touch with the ultimate love that we have for ourself and that IS ourself.

Not just our cells but our whole being and behaviour is a mix of divinely masculine and divinely feminine energies and traits, whether we are a male or a female human. In personality and type of behaviour, the divine masculine is the aspect of ourselves with drive and ambition, competitiveness, adventurousness and the ability to analyse logically and take action as a matter of survival. The divine feminine within us is the sensitive, nurturing, patient, flexible, gentle and receptive side, that is strongly in touch with feelings and intuition.

In the modern world women have been readjusting themselves to take on and express more and more of their divine masculine side. The pill swept along a massive social change, taking women from the kitchen to the boardroom . Once women were freed from eternal and repeated pregnancies and having to remain in a subservient or service role, they started to assert themselves and embrace their own inner untapped divine masculine side. As women adjusted to this inner rebalancing, some found themselves still haunted by their previous dominion, that of server, nurturer and supporter. Women now could go wherever they wanted, be whoever they wanted, do whatever they wanted without restriction. But in grabbing this newfound freedom with both hands some found themselves torn – wanting to race ahead yet still driven by the innate and long imprinted drive and duty to nurture and protect.

With the freedom to explore worlds, actions and careers that had till now been reserved for the males, some women carried deep inside a feeling of guilt or a need to prove their worth in this hitherto unavailable world. Coupled with this, the natural nurturing instinct and biology of mothering was still deeply imprinted within the female psyche. So these women started to push themselves harder and harder, to be the caretaker and nurturer of everything for everyone and in all situations.

I have met many women in today's world that have an inner message telling them they have to be **perfect** in order to earn their place. They must be the perfect student, the perfect partner, the perfect daughter, the perfect wife, the perfect mother, the perfect employee, the perfect employer, the perfect friend, in fact, taking on both the masculine and the feminine, but unable to blend them in a healthy way, they were becoming exhausted, either physically or emotionally, sometimes both. I have sensed that this over-stretching of limits, this ignoring of the inner voice telling them to rest, this belief that they were the one who had to push and push themselves way past exhaustion, to be one of the underlying causes of our current epidemic of breast cancer. In stepping into the impossible role of having to nurture the entire world, women have lost essential physical balance. The breast represents the female's giving and nurturing side, but that has become exhausted by the inability to say "no" and the need to be physically or metaphorically giving their care, their empathy, their devotion to every person and every situation.

Programmed to be always available for offspring, the newly evolving females found it hard to switch this off, leading them to physical and emotional depletion through pushing themselves to be available to everybody and everything all of the time. Eventually, trying to nurture every thing and every one in their sphere, the female's giving organ, the breast, becomes exhausted. Thus it stands to reason that it would then become out of balance, with the cells losing their natural healthy programmed patterns. In my long years as a healer I have noticed a common pattern in women who have succumbed to breast cancer. They cannot firmly, and without any excuses, say "No".

In this rapidly changing society it is vital to recognise where you have been trying to be all things to all people, where your buttons have been pushed and you've reached a stage of depletion by not protecting yourSELF. Take heed and learn to say "NO!". It is such a tiny word yet it proves to be so very hard for many women to utter. This is because the deep historical feminine programming to respond to all needs has not caught up with the modern world. Try it now, thrust your right arm out straight in front of you with your flat palm facing away, like a traffic cop, and firmly declare "NO!". Many women are surprised at how difficult this is, and when they try this exercise, the word "no" comes out in a small, unconvincing voice. They feel they don't have a right to deny anyone anything, so they push themselves way past the moment when they should have closed and protected their own space, their own body and their own spirit.

Even when these compulsive nurturers do say "no", is to quickly follow with a justification - an excuse or reason why they have had to say "no" at all, why they cannot be all things to all people. It is time to remember, you have a right to simply say 'no' to anyone at any time, without having to explain yourself. Nobody owns you but yourself, and if you do not respect and protect yourself, you will be of no use to anyone, anyway. So, try it again and with your right arm straight out in front of you, imagine someone asking you to do something and you're simply declaring "no" authoritatively and clearly. Do you see where that outstretched arm is attached to your body. Yes, you've got it, your breast! So you see, by saying 'no' firmly you may well be putting up a shield to protect your breast and keep it healthy.

Of course it is not just the women. Men have also had to make major adjustments to the changes in society and the shifting masculine/ feminine balance. As the women have been embracing their divine masculine, so the men have been shifting towards acknowledging their own inner divine feminine. Men today are far more involved with the upbringing of their children, with the household chores, with nurturing and tenderness, caring and sustaining, intuiting and empathising. Though they do not have breasts, they are experiencing their own transformation epidemic.

Traditionally men were to be the strong ones, to not give in to emotion, to stuff their feelings down and certainly not show them. After all, they had to shutdown and detach in order to stay on the battlefield or dispassionate and powerful enough to hunt dangerous prey. No wonder there has been such a rise in prostate cancer, as men battle with the call in their hearts to feel and express emotions which they have traditionally and for generations, had to avoid and stuff down. For their very survival, as soldiers and hunters, emotions were not allowed to surface, were indeed dangerous to pay attention to, as a matter of life and death. Even in the modern world without being involved in those professions it was still expected that a man would have a "stiff upper lip". Boys don't cry.

So gentlemen, just as the women must learn to say 'no', you must learn to say 'yes', a profound and inner yes to those feelings that have so long been suppressed. It is safe to allow them at last to rise to the surface, to be admitted to, to be shown and to be expressed in words and tears. You will not be killed by a mammoth, you will not be fired nor drummed out of the boys' club, you are in the modern world where all options are open to you and you will definitely and more wholly be a MAN if you develop a connection with and truly follow your feelings. And as for the prostate, it has been under so much pressure to hold those feelings back, to keep them down, to not allow them to travel up your body and into your heart, then into your mind and eventually into your tears of empathy and anguish. To keep that prostate healthy, perhaps it is time to listen carefully to your feelings, name them and express them whenever you wish to. By following the key process in Chapter 7, you will develop compassion and tenderness for your own wounds and allow them to have their say. This will lead to better health all round, mentally, spiritually, emotionally and physically.

FINDING THE EMOTIONAL CAUSE OF ILL HEALTH

Health problems are caused by imbalance. But what causes that balance to go out in the first place? There is a clear track and you can follow it like a detective when you work on healing yourself. It doesn't start in the body, but has to go through many processes to finally end in sickness, which is in fact the very last stage in a long chain of reactions. Ironically the imbalance that leads to ill health is all triggered by that primal, original fear, 'I won't get my milk and I am going to die'. So if that gut fear is not nipped in the bud, it moves to the next location, your mind. You think about, worry about an issue, try to solve it with logic and planning, but if it remains unresolved, then your emotions take over. That is the third stage, from spirit, to mind, to emotions until it reaches the last stage, the body.

It is interesting to take a rational look at which troubles may have triggered this sequence into a physical ailment. For example if you have a headache, perhaps you are thinking too hard, you are too full of worry. If you have a breathing problem, perhaps you don't feel welcome on the planet, a wound that may go all the way back to when you arrived here and took your first breath. If you have a stomach problem, perhaps there is a situation in your life you simply cannot stomach, or a bowel problem, something you can't process or express. Nose problem, someone is getting right up your nose. Hip problem, fear of taking that next big step forward, and so on. Once you unravel the original cause of the problem you can heal and reverse it, by dealing with that issue. In her comprehensive and compassionate book, Louise Hay goes into many emotional or original causes for ailments throughout the body. In my healing practice I have taken so many clients back in time to their childhood wounds, to unravel the real cause of this ultimate symptom of their spiritual and emotional suffering, a sickness. This unravelling is the precursor to the actual physical healing.

INNER HEALING MEDITATION

Quinto and I have spent many years as Shamanic healers, and a huge part of being able successfully heal our clients is trust. Trust in the outcome, trust in the beautiful and perfect design of our bodies, trust in our own cells' desire to be functioning optimally, trust in the ability and power of each person to put back into balance that which has gone out, in their own bodies, trust in the compassionate love innate in all beings, in the Creator and in the spark of God that resides in every one of us.

When we offer our guided healing sound bath, we teach our students how to reconnect with The Light and with their own body's cells. To bring the same Light that I encountered in my near-death experience, into, and thus realign, any cells that might be suffering or out of balance. To do this for yourself, it is so important to remember who you truly are, the person you were before you incarnated. Yes, you are supremely powerful and have complete mastery over your own life and your own body. Never forget, YOU are the commander of your ship, your cells serve and answer only to you, and all they want is to do everything they can to maintain your body in its most optimum condition for you.

Journeying to visit your cells.

If you cannot get to one of our workshops and would like to try the meditation of going within to connect with your cells, you can download the full event from our website. Meanwhile, here is a brief description of how to do it.

Find yourself a comfortable and quiet space. Make sure you will be undisturbed. Put on some soothing sounds or gentle instrumental music. Lie down, and breathe deeply and peacefully for a while as you completely let go and relax, knowing you are being held up by Mother Earth so there is nothing for you to do. Let all tension go. Remembering how you connect with the Light of unconditional love when doing your Daily Alignment, now visualise yourself drawing in that Light through your crown. Using your breath, visualise yourself going on a journey from your crown into and down through your own body, taking the Light with you so you can illuminate wherever you go. Allow yourself to observe, to inspect, to be the Captain visiting your cells, who have been loyal and worked tirelessly for you all through your life. They will be dancing with joy that you have come to visit and to acknowledge them.

As you observe how exquisitely beautiful and vibrantly colourful the inside of your perfectly designed body is, start to take a deeper look at individual cells. Travel down through your body, visiting each of the major organs. Notice if any cells seems to be lacking vibrance or not spinning properly. You will sense this as you observe them. With the power of the Light that you are bringing with you on this visit, touch each cell and see it illuminate and return to normal spin, full vibrancy.

If there has been pain in your body go and visit that place. Say to those cells "Thank you for alerting me to a problem, no need to continue with pain signals though, you are off duty as I will take it from here". You then go about the healing and repairing process of touching each cell with Light, until you are satisfied all that group of cells has been healed. Again, with acknowledgement and gratitude for all their tireless work on your behalf, you leave the cells you have been working on, moving to the next place you feel to go to. You can carry on this procedure for as long as you wish. Then, when you feel ready you can travel back up through your body to your crown, the entry-point where you began this journey, and come fully back into ordinary reality and full consciousness.

Having completed your healing journey to the cells inside your body you can open your eyes and notice how much better you feel, more in balance, more whole, more settled and more complete. You will most likely realise that the pain has gone, and feel that the process of repair that you have set in motion, is fully underway.

You can do this exercise as often as you wish, it is a wonderful way to take command of and self-heal any health issue that arises, or for general regular maintenance of the health of your loyal cells. You can find a download of our full guided meditation with our channelled music and chants at www.letinto.com.

Your body is the precious vehicle that transports your soul on all its adventures throughout your time on Earth. And as with any vehicle, it needs the right fuel and good maintenance. When we honour our own vehicle by exercising it gracefully and powerfully, and keeping it clean inside, we not only feel great, but we enjoy precious time in right relationship with our own body.

MIND HEALTH

"A healing is reinterpreting what you believe has happened to you"
Barbara Marciniak

If you find yourself consumed by worry, because you are dwelling on what might happen, with a sense of doom and gloom, here is a way to instantly turn yourself around, back into a positive state of mind. Remember, the past is no longer in existence, it is merely a memory in your head, a bunch of brain cells! Nor is the future here right now, it is simply a dream in your imagination, another bunch of dancing brain cells!. So the only actual reality is the present moment, the moment of NOW. Try saying out loud the word "now". You will realise that it only existed in that fractional moment when you said it and it has already gone into the past.

Here is the instant and surprisingly effective **trick you can use** whenever you need to cheer yourself up. When you feel down, depressed, when a dark cloud of hopelessness descends upon your consciousness, recognise that you have the power to bring out the sun again, immediately. You can actually flip a switch! All you have to do is remember that the only true reality is that fleeting moment of "now". Nothing else is true. So, for that split second of the **now** moment, choose JOY. It is not much to ask, it only takes less than a second, but you'll be amazed how it lights a tiny spark in the fire of your inner hope and tilts the axis of your mood straight back towards the positive. If the only true reality is the *now* moment, by choosing "joy" for that single moment you can break the spell you have been under. A spell which kept you trapped in the mire of too much dwelling in the non-reality of past or future. Why not give it a try right now, just for the next moment, choose "joy". See how uplifting that is?

So I invite you to spend more of your consciousness in the true reality of the present moment, the "now" moment. Then, by converting that single moment to "joy", you will be creating a wonderful past and a brilliant future.

Quinto likes to ask our clients this question. What is the most important thing in your life? After receiving the various answers he replies that **your attention** is the most important thing, because wherever you focus your attention, there you will create. Remember, attention plus intention equals creation. Where do you choose to focus your attention, today, now?

We are bombarded by the media with stories of tragedy, doom and gloom. Or we are enticed into viewing a drama in films or TV programmes, or perhaps screen games, that portray danger, horror and violence. Our brains and bodies then become confused, as the brain sees a trauma, the body tries to react to fear and shock with adrenaline yet we have to mentally override these signals by telling ourselves not to worry, there isn't really any danger because it is not real, just a screen. Meanwhile the damage has only just begun. We have taken into our mental landscape things that are ugly or frightening and no matter how much we try to rationalise, our body will react, and most likely our brain will replay the horror later in a natural bid to solve the problem. This is why people passing a traffic accident slow down and gawp. In slang parlance this is known as 'rubber necking', as if humans get some kind of a kick out of viewing others' misfortune and suffering. But the real reason we need to check out in as much detail as possible what exactly happened here, is so that we can avoid a similar misfortune. We look for data to save and protect ourselves from the same fate. We need to watch, to understand and to solve to stay out of danger. The producers of dramas play into this, which is why we go on needing to view them. But the longterm effect on your body and mind is destructive. It may not seem so at the time but the more dark and negative input is absorbed into the cerebral cortex compelling us to resurrect our primal and original fears, the further we travel from the healthy and compassionate state of love and balance, that is physical and mental health.

We are sensitive and beautifully designed beings. We function perfectly if we put the right fuel in that runs our motor smoothly. When put the wrong fuel, such as junk food or poisons such as alcohol and recreational drugs, into our beautiful vehicle it is like owning a petrol driven rolls royce and putting drops of diesel into the tank. The engine will not run smoothly, we will lose momentum and the joy of our beautiful vehicle running at optimum capacity, and if we put enough diesel into the tank, the whole vehicle will seize up totally. Not just our bodies but also our minds need the right fuel, and that best fuel is to be found by taking time in nature. Our minds and our bodies then slow to their natural pace, we feel elated through the joy of connection and right fuel input. Our vehicle, from head to toe, gets a boost from the top quality fuel that keeps it running in positivity and joy.

Be compassionate and kind to yourself. Compassion and kindness come naturally to us humans if fear is put on the back burner. Thus, another great food for the mind and soul is giving and the sharing of your innate compassion for those less fortunate than yourself. To find a cause, a situation where you can work alongside others to help and heal and restore balance on the planet, you find your mood instantly elevated. If your mind is full of woe, a belief in powerlessness or full of resentment, a belief in being wronged, full of anxiety in the belief of being the only responsible one or full of sorrow, in the belief that you are alone and unsupported, then that is what you will create.

When you change your attention, you change what you create. If your attention is on truth and gratitude, love and sincerity, honesty and kindness, authenticity and respect, then you will create a healthy and authentic life for yourself, sending a balanced energy out into the world too.

It is in our design, for our happiness and fulfilment, that we need to spend time simply being creative. It is in such moments, immersed in our art or music, that we are living in the present moment, not paying attention to the mental chatter of either past or future events, just simply being. Meditation or shamanic journeying are tools you can use to bring you, in the present moment, to your deepest self, your power and your higher mind.

From the teachings in Chapter 7, you will remember that all feelings that are not love, come from fear, and that the fear is held by your wounded inner child pieces. When you see a child having a tantrum, they are expressing their fear through panic and anger. Or, if all roads to expressing their fear are closed, they will withdraw into silent depression. Thus it is with us as adults, when our kingdom is lost and being run by a frightened child we can find ourselves having angry outbursts or becoming depressed. Depression is unexpressed anger, and anger is unexpressed fear. So the key to lifting the cloud of depression is to go to the source, your wounded child's terror, and unravel the trauma, stepping up as the wise sovereign to give this frightened little one the reassurance and comfort he or she has been aching for. By taking care of this little one you will step back into control of your life while having a very valuable purpose – to take care of your wounded child pieces one by one, hearing their stories and giving them support, nurturing and reassuring them. After all, poor helpless little things, who else can they turn to? Also, by stepping into the essential role of 'parenting' these lost children, you find true value and purpose while healing your mind and soul. This way your fears subside.These practices can provide a natural high which is innately yours and provides a wonderful bridge to your own body, mental strength and universal wisdom. On the contrary, the high that is imposed on your body and mind by drugs or alcohol, is a high that takes rather than gives. It removes you from your innate power and wisdom, and gives it all away to the plant or the substance, thus weakening you in mind, body, soul and spirit, causing a downward spiral into sickness and imbalance.

The key to your health is in you. The key to maintaining a state of loving balance through all aspects of your life is also within you. You do have the power to overcome the fear that drives all physical and mental imbalance if you stay alert to your feelings, then keep using the techniques described above, and to maintain that balance, give yourself the gift of practicing your Daily Alignment as described in Chapter 6. Doing all these things every day is life-changing because when committed to they can return you to your true, authentic loving and balanced self. And then......the world is your oyster!

CHAPTER 10

Opposites

AN OPEN MIND AND AN OPEN HEART MAKE LIFE THE FUN
ADVENTURE IT WAS ALWAYS MEANT TO BE

So far this book has been full of serious digging and delving, and profound techniques which, if you practice them, will improve your life. Now it is time for some fun, a little breather of lightheartedness with the game of opposites. This makes your mind more fluid and reminds you it can be fun to step away from set patterning and form, into an Aquarian Age way of innovation, breaking outdated moulds and challenging the 'known'. Let's be controversial, free ourselves from the prison of assumptions and embrace the possibility that **EVERYTHING JUST MIGHT BE THE OPPOSITE OF WHAT IT SEEMS**

I don't know when I first played with this idea, but it started as I began to realise that life and people can actually be quite the opposite of what they appear to be, a contradiction of what we have been lead to believe, if viewed from a completely different angle. It is so refreshing to allow one's mind to step away from it's ingrained rut and restrictions. I've always been someone who liked to challenge the rules, haven't you? Once you get started with this game of seeing what you thought you knew from a completely different perspective, all kinds of realisations and revelations will come to you, encouraging you to convert limitation into limitless possibilities in all aspects of your life.

It is all too easy to get locked into a paradigm of beliefs or certainties, paralysed by the fear of stepping away from them. Often these beliefs are trained into us by the authority figures in our early lives – our parents, teachers, caretakers or priests. This causes our minds to calcify, to get stuck in a rigid paradigm, outside of which is some perceived drama or disaster, so we stay limited and imprisoned through fear.

One such realisation of opposites jumped out at me when I recognised my shyness and resistance to standing up in front of people was in fact a huge ego trip! I was engrossed in the self-absorbed obsession that I might be judged or I would not look right or that my words would come out wrong. Thus I resisted for several weeks the prodding from my guides to teach what I knew. The breakthrough came when I awoke one morning to the realisation that I was completely stuck in my ego, which was holding me frozen in it's thrall. Sharing my knowledge wasn't all about whether I'd sink or swim, make a fool of myself or be ridiculed, because it wasn't about the little ME. It was about being wise enough and empty enough to step aside and permit. To simply allow the teachings to flow through me to those who would benefit from hearing them. This was a profound turning point. I suddenly saw that shyness or self-consciousness is a terrible block to the fulfilment of our innate gifts, as it was a totally self-centred viewpoint.

As a shamanic healer I had learned that the more I stepped aside and allowed the healing gifts to flow through me, the more powerful and potent the healing would always be for my client. I was already adept at this stepping aside and allowing channelling while giving a healing or a reading. In such moments I was in another zone. Only later did I realise I could apply that 'stepping aside and allowing' to any aspect of my life where my ego threatened to hamper me. It was another way to ignore the sabotaging reproval from my internalised critical parent.

From this life-changing revelation of shyness actually being an ego trip, I decided that Mick Jagger strutting across the stage with his chest puffed out was the opposite of an ego trip, it was actually wholehearted giving. I began to experiment with other ingrained concepts. By turning them on their head too, this became a phenomenal game as well as a valuable tool for opening my mind to a much broader perspective on human behaviours. So as I share this idea with you, allow it to lighten your load, open up your life and take you away from dogmatic restrictions. The opposite of what you thought. Why not try it on for size?

See yourself sitting in a room gazing at the blank wall in front of you. You have been told by an anxious and irrationally fearful authority figure that it is your duty to simply stare at that wall, and that to get up or to turn around would be utterly selfish, certainly foolish. The authority figure walks out, leaving you dutifully staring at the wall. There is no-one to keep you rooted to that spot now, except the infection of another's fear which has restricted your life experience. So that becomes your world, all you know of life is that chair and that dull wall.

But supposing you dare to trust your own intuition, to use your initiative and your free will to break free from the fear-driven imposed containment. Suppose you listen to your inner voices of reason and curiosity, above the imposed voice of fear, and with a courageous effort you stand up, turn around and look behind you. To your relief nothing bad happens, instead you see a window. Intrigued, you take the courage to walk over to that window and you are amazed. How astonishing is the picture that unfolds before your eyes, a whole world that existed out there which you couldn't have even imagined if you'd followed someone else's meaningless, fear-driven imprisonment. Now you can see fields, trees, beautiful flowers and blue sky, perhaps a sparkling stream, none of which would have graced your thoughts had you not decided to take off your mental blindfold, take the risk of viewing life from a whole new perspective, outside of the box of others' imposed rigidity. You would realise that you had assumed the world to be one thing when in truth it was much bigger and more full of beauty and diversity than you could have ever imagined. Some courage to step beyond the externally imposed and self-perpetuating boundaries, to look at life from a completely new perspective, is all it takes. It is one more way of silencing those inner critics, the power-hungry 'advisors'.

Open your mind, imagine that ANYTHING is possible, and nothing is set in stone. It is such a joy to take your life into your own hands, and make all the fear-driven restrictions into flexible possibilities. This way, life can be whatever you want it to be because in fact YOU are creating it moment by moment. Have fun and embrace the idea that any truth you currently believe may be hiding another idea, which may in fact be the real truth. This game can make life lighter, brighter and quite often hilarious when you realise how blinkered you and others have been! Treat it as a game, and remember, you are a free, inquisitive and perfect soul who does not have to take on board or get bogged down by anybody else's beliefs, including mine!

Here are a some reminders of opposites from earlier chapters, plus some new ones. If you like, you can put the word "maybe" in front of each:

1. Never forgive.
2. Shyness, guilt and worry are ego trips.
3. Money is love.
4. There are no victims.
5. There are no villains.
6. There are no problems.
7. There is no past nor future.
8. Being selfish is considerate.
9. It is healthy to worship a certain image.
10. It is not a sin to eat meat.
11. There are no endings nor beginnings.
12. Embrace the worst.

1. NEVER FORGIVE ANYONE

Remember this one from an earlier chapter? I was taught that forgiveness makes us benevolent and generous of spirit. However I became aware that when we put ourselves in this righteous position we perpetuate an unending dance with the 'wrong doer'. This was such a big revelation. I realised that if I was to forgive, as taught by my peers, I had first to sit in judgement, placing the perpetrator far beneath me because I was judging them as "wrong" or "bad" and myself as "right"eous. Internally I told myself that despite the fact that they had done wrong, I would bestow upon them the gift of my forgiveness. How arrogant I was, sitting high above them in a state of superior benevolence. But by doing this I realised that no matter how much I desired to let go of the negative energy attached to the incident, there could be no closure so long as I continued to judge them. I would never rid myself of the attachments to this 'crime' because I would always consider myself to be the victim and they, the criminal, putting us on two very different levels. Thus my power was lost as I had given it and plenty of my precious energy away, to judgement. So to achieve closure, I realised I had to turn the whole episode on its head and see the gift this tough experience had brought to me, the gift of learning. Then, instead of having to try to forgive the person I simply thanked them. Why?

Looking back over the issue I could see how I did suffer, but I could also see how that period of suffering moulded me, pushed me, shaped me. How I gained in knowledge and understanding as a result of that struggle or hurt. In fact, this perpetrator was actually a helper as they had facilitated my advancement in understanding and compassion.

Going deeper still, which meant taking my power back and closing the chapter forever, I took full responsibility by acknowledging that my soul must have called this lesson to me in the first place, that I was in charge and that the perpetrator was only doing my soul's bidding by placing themselves in the role of provocateur. It was a performance I had cast them in and they had agreed to play on the stage of my life, an agreement made aeons ago. By putting them and yourself on an equal level, as souls, you are now able to close the chapter with no remaining attachments. With the recognition that I was and always have been in charge, I was able to let the incident go and reclaim both my power and my compassion.

2. GUILT and WORRY are HUGE EGO TRIPS

Many people are riddled with guilt about things they've done or not done. Parents in particular 'beat themselves up' about not being good enough, not doing enough, not managing to be *perfect*. In all aspects of your life, opportunities arise for you to spend time fretting and worrying, or for you to fall into feelings of guilt or shame. So here is a tool to help you rid yourself of these energy-sucking pastimes. I offer you this example of something that happened in my own life.

I was nearly home, driving up the steep hill when I noticed an old lady lugging two heavy bags of shopping up the road. My mind said "I should stop and offer her a lift" but I sailed past. Once home, I sat comfortably with a cup of tea and my mind started up this dialogue ..."I should have stopped for that poor old lady, I feel terribly guilty, I am not a very nice person, I really feel ashamed of myself" and so on. How many times did I say "I". How did that help the lady on the hill? My worry, shame and guilt helped no-one. It certainly did not change the world for the better. In fact it was a total self-indulgence.

So you might listen to that inner voice of compassion that prompts you, then take right action, but if you don't, then let it go, confident in the fact that it was not your job that time. Don't waste energy with your ego going over and over what YOU could or might have done. Simply **do your best then leave the rest**. By recognising that you did your best and by respecting the fact that each other human on the planet is walking their own chosen path, that it is not your job to fix them or rescue them, then you can live in harmony with yourself and with the rest of creation. And by adopting the phrase "**My best is good enough**" you let go of the time and energy wasting ego-trips of guilt and worry. Exercise compassion, for YOURSELF. You haven't failed, you aren't bad, you simply did your best. How can you do more than that? It also helps you to be less judgemental and more compassionate if you consider that other people are also only doing their best. Guilt and worry are, in truth, those conniving advisors undermining your kingdom. Silence them and have the utmost compassion for the one who truly needs your help – your inner wounded child.

3. MONEY IS LOVE

As mentioned in the chapter about money, we are taught "money is the root of all evil". How often are we led to feel guilt about money? Money is dirty and to want it is shameful. Yet I was given quite a different perspective by being shown that if our money was gained in recognition of our creating what we love to create, money would be the representation or symbol of love. In some cases it already is.

This is especially so when a person is doing what they love to do. For example, if I love to make jewellery or paint pictures or carve wooden objects, maybe I even love to tidy, clean and make order, when I devote myself to a task I am giving it my love. So when I am paid money for that object or task, what is being paid for is my love. I take that money and pay for something that has also been made from the energy of love, thus the money is just a love exchange all the way down the line.

Many people spend their lives in compromise, doing a job that brings necessary money, despite the fact that they do not feel inspired by what they do. In this case it ceases to be love, it becomes drudgery. The bright energy of love becomes dulled and the money becomes a symbol of discontent. It is then used to compensate for the self-sacrificing and life disappointments by purchasing objects, *things* that can justify the sacrifice and are a substitute for the love we yearn for. "I may have slaved away at a job I hate, but at least I can afford that new shiny object which I have been told, by advertisers, will make me feel better and will fill the empty spaces inside of me, showing the world I have value". When money becomes a thing to chase after, it is always just out of reach. Chase the money, it eludes you. However, the opposite is true when you take the path of joy. Because when you truly follow your dreams, the money chases you. If money is a flowing river of love, it doesn't stay with you, it simply flows through you and on to the next person. When money becomes used for gain with no consideration for the damaging effects on human life and dignity, it becomes a vehicle for corruption, thus the river becomes polluted and those drinking the water beyond it will be 'poisoned'.

So, if you cease to chase the money but simply immerse yourself in the pure spark and natural creation of what you LOVE to do, the money will increasingly chase you! This is because you will put so much love into what you do that others will want it, seek it, and pay for it. That is an exchange of love. That is a healthy way to see and treat money, isn't it?

4. THERE ARE NO VICTIMS

Victimhood is a lie. Nothing lands randomly in someone's lap making them into a victim. Each one of us has ultimate power over our lives and the outcome of our behaviour and attitudes. When we believe ourselves to be a victim, we give our power away and remain weak. Of course there will be times in each of our lives when we experience heartbreak and tragedy, and yes we will receive loving support at those times. Yet it is vital to recognise that nothing happens by chance because way back before you incarnated you originally CHOSE all your life events as part of your learning and the growing of your own Light, compassion and love. Remember, in your own life, only by living through a tragedy and experiencing it first hand can you truly develop empathy for others when they go through something similar.

5. THERE ARE NO VILLAINS

There are no villains, only frantic infants, terrified they will not get their milk, so out of fear they behave in a dastardly way. Next time you encounter a bully, recognise that their kingdom is being entirely run by a wounded, frightened little internalised child from their own past. Yet, because you weren't there when they were growing up, experiencing life through their young eyes, you will never be able to fix them or their problem. But you do have the right to speak up, thus protecting and championing your own inner wounded child and defending your kingdom.

The best way to change a despot, to open his heart, is to teach him how to release and heal the inner fears that drive him to behave so uncaringly. If you wish to change the harmful ways of a world leader or industry magnate, send the most powerfully transformative tool in the universe, LOVE, with the intention that they may release their inner fears and reconnect with their divine essence of love and compassion. You can do this solo or get together with a group of like-minded people who will quietly and compassionately direct that loving and healing energy towards the target. Thus you will be working from love and with love, and as you know, there is no 'weapon' in the universe more potent. The human that learns to tend to their own fears and wounds by listening to their internalised frightened child pieces and caring for them with compassion and love, will never become a villain nor a despot.

One other point about villains. Sometimes when blaming another person's behaviour for our suffering, we need also to be grateful for the power of the lesson they have taught us, even it it is to clarify what we definitely will not tolerate nor welcome into our life bullying behaviour. Remember the possibility that you already requested they play this particular role on the stage in your life of bringing the very discomfort you needed in order to grow and learn, and reclaim your power. Thus instead of being an actual villain, their soul may even have made a huge sacrifice to play the bad guy just to facilitate the learning you requested before incarnation. Now that is really turning things on their head, isn't it?

6. THERE ARE NO PROBLEMS

There are no problems, only opportunities. Opportunities to learn and grow. So when you hit an issue, don't let fear swamp you and blind you. Before panic or overwhelm blot out your rationality, rather than saying 'I' am furious or insulted, teach yourself to shift into saying 'he' or 'she' (your inner wounded child) is feeling furious or insulted, or whatever the emotion is. Thus you externalise the feeling and by being detached you can see clearly enough to decipher where the wound from your earliest days is causing a reaction in the here and now, then resolve it through compassion and support for that wounded little version of yourself. Using the tools and techniques given, you can calmly and maturely tackle the problem, remembering you chose it for a reason. Thus the 'problem' converts into an opportunity for growth and enlightenment, as all problems are truly here to do.

7. THERE IS NO PAST nor FUTURE

'Past' and 'future' are both concepts in your mind. Remember from the previous chapter, the past is just a memory, a bunch of brain cells in fact. The future isn't here yet, it is just a dream, another bunch of brain cells. Thus, the only true reality is the present moment. With this realisation, spend some time each day simply enjoying BEING instead of racing around DOING. Those things that frightened the younger you, in the past, are no longer here. Only the fear attached to them can travel to the present. Thus as the compassionate and mature sovereign you are today, you have the power to heal them.

8. BEING SELFISH IS CONSIDERATE

The more you look into your own issues, the more you take care of your own wounded inner child and the more you follow your heart, doing what YOU love to do, the happier and more balanced you will be. This will reflect joyfully and positively on everyone around you as in taking your own power back and ceasing to blame or expect, you soothe and empower all around you. Spending time going within to REMEMBER WHO YOU TRULY ARE will result in you sharing your true gifts with the world.

9. IT CAN BE HEALTHY TO WORSHIP AN IMAGE

Many religions, including the Bible, teach us not to worship craven images, and not to put our faith in a physical model that we believe holds the power of God. I interpret this less as a disrespect of God, more as a disrespect of ourselves, of the god within each of us. When a person looks at, for example, a cross or a statue of the Buddha, they feel a connection with the Divine even though they know that the piece of wood or ceramic they are gazing at does not hold the power. It is merely a trigger to induce that sacred connection. But here is an image you might healthily worship, knowing it does hold the power. An image of yourself as a child. What if your altar were to have as it's centrepiece a photo of you as an infant, or pictures of you as a child, alongside a picture of you right now, as an adult. Kept sacred and respected, those images would remind you of your compassion, your own sacred divinity and the purpose of your journey, taking you back to realising that YOU ARE A SPARK OF GOD. Surely if each of us kept THAT image sacred and sincerely respected, it would benefit all of mankind.

10. IT MIGHT NOT BE A CRIME TO EAT MEAT

Emotive and maybe taking you out of your comfort zone, especially if you are a vegan, it is interesting to play with this controversial concept. Or for those of you who feel the need to consume animal products (you are probably blood type 'O') then this will help you let go of the guilt. Not everybody feels the desire to eat meat, but for those who do, let's start by remembering that nothing in life stays the same, everything is in a constant state of transformation. The Shaman knows that everything has spirit and that spirit has free will. Ancient tribal people held all of nature in high regard. When hunting for food, they honoured the animal that would sacrifice its life to offer its many gifts for the tribe's sustainment. Those people lived within and utterly dependent upon nature for their survival. They also recognised that all of nature was inter-dependent and equal. They deeply understood the concept of giving and sharing, and did not see themselves as superior to any creature or aspect of the natural world.

The indigenous people of the Pacific Northwest understood a great deal about giving. There were regular gift-giving gatherings at which the goal was to give away as much as possible, to others. Their Potlatch ceremonies were called the great 'give away', where beautifully beaded moccasins, woven blankets, quilled belts, and many precious items that they had spent months crafting were given as gifts to people from other tribes who had come to the gathering. When leaving, it was considered shameful if you had received more than you had given. Equally the sun and rain from the heavens, the plants that healed, the buffalo that supplied tribal people with meat, clothing, shelter blankets and so much more, were seen as a great giving, and they in return wished to give back with gratitude and to maintain the balance. It is hard for our modern attitude of 'What can I get?' to understand the ancient ways of balance which meant living utterly connected with the sources of existence in a paradigm of 'What can I give?'.

Some years ago when I was running a workshop I went deep into the countryside with my students. We came upon a steep ridge and high above us majestic hawks were circling and hunting. On the hillside around us were many rabbits grazing, which, as we came closer, anxiously scurried away. In my shamanic tradition the rabbit represents fear and anxiety while the hawk represents the ability to distance oneself from a problem and gain perspective. In that moment I suddenly received a new insight too. It came to me in a flash that if one of these timid and fear-filled rabbits were to be consumed by a hawk, they would become the hawk and then see life through the eyes of that hawk. Thus they would be able to experience a whole different existence, soaring majestically above their previous life, with a completely new perspective. So I ceased to feel sorry for the rabbits as potential victims of the hawk circling above. Instead I saw the one who was eaten by a hawk as having sought that transformation into feeling the joy of flying and seeing life from a hawk's eyes high up in the sky.

Was it possible therefore, that the particular buffalo that was slain and whose meat was eaten by the tribe, had chosen to experience life as a human? Native American people did understand the concept of transition as they did not bury their dead but put them up on platforms to be consumed by and transformed into, the circling crows, thus taking on the crow's form and seeing the world from its eyes. Whether we eat meat, plants, grains or seeds, we are eating that which has been alive and it's life sustains our life. Plants, too, sacrifice themselves for human consumption. As with the hawk offering the rabbit a chance to experience life as a hawk, so the human can offer whichever animal or plant they eat, the chance to live for a while in the human body and see life from the human's eyes. Respecting its spirit while thanking it for the food it has offered, ancient people recognised that an animal's sacrifice for our benefit is an exchange, a balance, not a one sided victim perpetrator event. It is not shameful to eat meat, only shameful to treat any creature of plant with disrespect or cruelty. In order for us to respect each other and the creatures with which we share this Earth, let us honour each other with dignity, kindness and consideration. We know plants are sensitive and reactive, so even the vegan must become aware of the spirit of the plant they will consume, thanking it for giving its life and offering it the opportunity to see life from human eyes.

11. THERE ARE NO ENDINGS nor BEGINNINGS

When I was young, contemplating how vast the universe was, the following idea sparked in me. Supposing the words 'ending' and 'beginning' were simply made up by humans to explain birth and death, but in reality were merely concepts, because in fact neither ending nor beginning actually existed? From my near-death experience I was clearly shown that after we die we are reborn, so our souls are on a circular journey, one ending becoming the next beginning. Humans are very attached to the concept of things having a start and a finish, and scientists wonder where the cosmos ends, but what if it doesn't? Certainly they see from the tiniest particles they have managed to analyse, that everything is in a perpetual motion of transformation. I like to play with the idea that, if we as humans simply made up the concepts of beginnings and endings, then maybe the universe does go on FOREVER, as do we. Rather than starts and finishes, perhaps there are simply transformations.

12. EMBRACE THE WORST THAT MIGHT HAPPEN

This is a great game you can play when you experience dread or have reached a stalemate from fearing an outcome. It is like a board game and you move in a circular pattern round the board. Imagine it's a lily pond and you, the frog, will hop to the next lily pad with each answer.

So you are afraid to do something. Whatever it is, start playing the game by asking yourself "What's THE WORST THAT COULD HAPPEN if I do this?" When the answer comes, hop to the next lily pad and ask the question again.

Let's play the game with an example. Imagine for a moment that you are alone and isolated and have a great fear to step into a relationship.

Q. "What's the worst that could happen if I stepped into a relationship?"

Now listen for the answer, it might be something like this...

A. *"I might be let down again"*

Move to the next lily pad, it has that name *I might be let down again,* on it.
Then ask yourself...

Q. "What's the worst that could happen if I was let down?"

Listen for the answer, it might be...

A. *"I might get hurt"*

Move to the next lily pad which has that name on it.
As you continue it goes something like this.

Q. "What's the worst that could happen if I got hurt?"

A. *"I might lose my trust"* . Move to the next lily pad.

Q. "What's the worst that could happen if I lost my trust?"

A. *"I might shut down my heart"* .Move to the next lily pad.

Q "What's the worst that could happen if I shut down my heart?"

A. *"I' would be isolated and alone"*

BINGO! You've come full circle and arrived back to where you started, you are actually there right now, IN the worst that can happen!

What you have just been shocked to discover, by playing this game, is that the very worst that can happen if you stepped forward into your fear, is that you would end up exactly where you are right now. In other words, THERE IS NO WORSE THAT CAN HAPPEN. Because the very, very worst that could happen is here, with you already at this moment.

So here's the gold in this game. By realising there is no worse that can happen it becomes OK to step forward, because the ultimate outcome is no worse than where you started, but by stepping forward you just might, and most likely will, open the door to SOMETHING BETTER. So the risk is no risk at all.

If you analyse the whole situation further you come to realise that your own fear of being imprisoned has already got you held captive. It's beautifully ironic isn't it? Here are some of the most common fears people harbour, that can be melted away by playing this game.

Fear of being in a relationship (or falling in love)
Fear of being trapped
Fear of being squashed (ridiculed or judged)
Fear of being alone
Fear of being ugly
Fear of being a failure
Fear of rejection
Fear of encountering a creature (for example, spider)
Fear of being damaged

Whatever your fear, by playing the game called 'What's The Worst That Could Happen If..." you recognise that the outcome will inevitably be far better than your dread has led you to imagine.

AND THE WORST THAT CAN HAPPEN IF YOU CHALLENGE ASSUMPTIONS IS...?

Finger-wagging condemnation? Who is that in your psyche...yes, you guessed it, your internalised critical parents. Those advisors hold us back, so put them firmly in their place. You are not here to be hampered by judgement, you are here to play with life and enjoy liberation. So have fun challenging assumptions and dogma, it may just set you free!

By keeping your mind open to all possibilities and by trying out the concept of reality being the opposite of what you had come to believe, you stay flexible and adventurous instead of brittle and stuck in a rut or calcified by judgement. Classic physical symptoms of this are stiff joints, arthritis, tension. By continuing to open your mind to see whether your beliefs have become stale and rigid, have crystallised or become ingrained, you can once again see how to flexibly flow with life instead of fighting against it.

If we try viewing everything we have been led to believe from its opposite perspective, there is a liberation from the control and finger-wagging warnings of the fearful. If we become conscious and wise we will cease to do things in a way that is care-less, but will do things in a way that is care-full. In order for humans to be fulfilled and driven by love instead of fear; in order for this planet to be run by the greatest power of the universe, Love, then a good place to start is with the turning of what you 'know' upside down to take a look at it from a completely different perspective, and play with that. There is no right nor wrong, only an opening of consciousness and a release of judgement, to become wise in love and joyful in knowing.

CHAPTER 11
Remember Your Perfection

Over a lifetime of preparing thousands upon thousands of astrology charts, which are personality and life choice maps, there is one thing I know for certain. We are all equal. The gifts and challenges may be distributed differently for each person, but at the end of the day it all amounts to 100 per cent. Because I have never seen a chart of a person who was 90 per cent nor one who was 110 percent, it is simply impossible.

I like to use the analogy of the 'pick-n-mix', where you have lots of different sweets of all shapes, sizes and flavours to choose from. Holding your bag, you lift each flap making your choices about which ones and how many of them you would like. Six of these, three of those, one of this type, five of that sort and so on, making your personal selection from all the varieties on offer until you have exactly what YOU desire. This is how it is with your personal and specific choices for your new lifetime. You choose your own mix before you incarnate, and it is uniquely yours. You and I and all humans have the same weight allowance in our 'Pick and Mix' bag, yet we each make a different selection. We are all equal and we are all dancing together in the game of life, as one. We have each made our individual choices and are walking our own chosen path and the glorious thing is, we can choose every day to enjoy a lifetime of fun and respect for each others' choices.

I see humanity as a huge jigsaw puzzle, and each human one piece of that puzzle, unique in colour, shape and size, that makes the picture work. When my children were teenagers I saw them and their friends going through that familiar insecure phase we all went through at that stage in our development. A time when we believed others held the key to our perfection, our acceptance, our being 'good enough' to be part of the human race. I noticed them doing what we have all done in our youth, and some of us still do, trying to copy or emulate someone outside of themselves, a hero or a star, rather than seeing their own innate and unique excellence. These teenagers looked at their peers or their heroes and tried to become them, not realising they were completely ideal just as they were.

As I saw them going through this insecure struggle I would explain that the colour, shape and size of their particular jigsaw piece, their 'self', was absolutely perfect just as it was. I pointed out that if they changed one piece in a jigsaw puzzle to copy or become more like a different piece, there would be nowhere for that piece to now fit and the whole puzzle would be ruined. I found this to be a great way of visualising why each of us is exactly right just as we are, different from rather than a clone of the next person, and that difference in each of us jigsaw pieces, when put together, creates the masterpiece that is humanity.

The teenager is searching for their identity before they slide into adulthood. However this elusive 'self' they seek cannot be found in the plastic perfection of a film star or sports hero, as the self they unconsciously seek is their TRUE self, their core identity, the person they were before they incarnated and adapted. That is our exquisite and exactly right self, the one who we can go back through the maze to find, if we possess the tools.

So as ever, the solution we seek to our lostness and confusion at any age is never to be found 'out there', but can only be re-discovered and re-kindled from deep 'within here'. REMEMBER WHO YOU TRULY ARE. That is, the person in your core and who you always were prior to coming to Earth. To remember who you truly are you must track your way back to before, to your essence. Therein lies your exquisite perfection.

MESSAGES FROM SPIRIT

I receive visions and knowledge from my guides and my higher self. How can you plug into that source and receive direct downloads yourself? First of all it is important to recognise your perfection which means that you are already tuned. Secondly you need to remove barriers of fear and unworthiness by simply stepping into complete trust, as described in the chapter on manifesting. Allow the beautiful messages to naturally drift in. If it helps, think of it as merely your intuition working in technicolour! If you imagine something harsh, dark or ugly, that is simply a manifestation of your own fear and means it is time to talk with your wounded child again, to hear what frightened them when they were little, to reassure them that all the spirits outside of us are benevolent and kind. Fear and terrifying spectres are not part of the benevolent spirit world, they dwell only in the horrors of childhood trauma.

People ask me about plant spirit medicines, such as Ayahuasca. They have their place in healing provided they are not treated as recreational or something to tick off on your bucket list. Most importantly of all, as the name implies, plants have spirits. Some of these offer to help and enlighten us, but only when they are treated with the utmost respect, with due ceremony performed by a sincere and well trained indigenous shaman with inherited wisdom and a relationship with the spirit of that plant, in the location where it naturally grows. Only then, and only if your soul truly needs the healing this plant offers.

Tobacco leaf was very sacred to the Native American people, who had a deep spiritual tradition with their pipe ceremony. That ceremony was as reverent and important as holy communion has been for Christians. During the filling of the pipe bowl with sacred tobacco many prayers would be offered to Mother Earth, Grandfather Sun, the spirits of the four directions and the ancestors. Then the pipe was passed with humility and respect, in a very specific, traditional manner, the smoke would be taken into the mouth reverently, but not inhaled! It was simply puffed out and up to Great Spirit as a vehicle for the transmission of prayer. The use of tobacco as a recreational drug came to the west as a result of ignorance and thus a lack of respect for the spirit of the tobacco plant and it's offered use for prayer.

...Tobacco, sacred once, now kills
Where native spirits roamed the hills
And sugar, wrenched from slaving brow
Creates an epidemic now...

This poem came through me after an experience when my children were young. We had just finished dinner when our visiting relative lit up a cigarette at the table. I asked politely if he would mind going outside to smoke. Suddenly he slammed his fist down on the table and shouted "I am free...to smoke where and when I want!" My mind reeled at this outburst, but what immediately came to me was, "The opposite is true". He was far from free, he had a ball and chain around his ankle, because the tobacco owned him and he was its slave, giving his health and his cash to it on a daily basis.

Using substances to get high or for recreational purposes is not only unnecessary, it will harm rather than heal as. While pretending to give power and insight, it steals your power and blurs your true, inner vision. This is because the experience you have will not be yours, it will belong to the spirit of the plant or product you have consumed which is happy to take you and your power away, to energetically feed of you and deplete you in fact. So instead of gaining you are giving away vital power and wisdom.

Many people over the centuries have also given their power away by attributing their awareness or 'enlightenment' to gurus, saints or items, instead of going to the greatest source of all, the SELF. The search in the bottle, the smoke or the drug, is truly a search to find that elusive track back to the Light, the place from whence we came and which we miss like crazy. The 'coming home' that we crave in our deepest essence is so intangible yet we know it will make us feel complete, connected and bathed in the most divine love - our source. That CAN be achieved, and is most beautifully and safely built day by day, by practicing your Daily Alignment.

We spend a lifetime seeking to return, torn between the awareness that we are living a divine learning opportunity here on Earth and the desire to get back to the source. Wavering between the consciousness that we are lucky to have received a place at this University of divine learning, and the longing to reconnect, we seek ways to overcome the aching loneliness of separation. Some fill that with relationships here on Earth, or with religion. Of course those relationships are vital and valuable but inevitably the truth is we are each an independent and empowered soul travelling separately on our journey of learning, and while a relationship with another human can be utterly beautiful, it will not take you back to the source of your being. Only YOU can do that. By doing the Daily Alignment you will experience a supremely healthy and self-empowering way to make that reconnection.

ADAPTED CORE IDENTITY

In Chapter 4, I explained that we form an original persona when we come to Earth, in order to fit in, adapt, survive. Then we cling onto that persona as if it were a life-raft, not realising when it is no longer useful.

We arrive on earth, we find our place, we learn compromises and are told who we are and who we are not, by authority figures. Thus, by the age of six we have developed a constructed belief about who we are. It is how we slot into the world that we have found ourselves in. I call that identity the 'I'M THE ONE THAT'. It adapts us away from our original, innate SELF, and this adaptation starts just before we are born. This dysfunctional identity relates to several things. How can I survive? How can I find a place where I fit into the family group? How can I cope with all the influences around me? It is a constructed and manipulated persona, taken on and worn like a suit, in order to carry on.

Inevitably that identity is dysfunctional as it is coloured by our fear-based wounds. Yet, as we grow older we carry on believing ourselves to be that adapted identity formed in early childhood. Though it is not our true, authentic self, it is who we have convinced ourself to be, so it becomes the only identity we know. Even when the identity is dysfunctional, we cling onto it, we'd be lost without it. That is why, as adults, we unwittingly keep creating situations in our lives that will take us back to and re-confirm that we are indeed THAT persona. It may not be a very happy persona and we don't hang onto it because we LIKE the pain of that contrived state. We cling onto it because it is the only identity we know and the person we had to adapt into being, in order to stay here on Earth, or so we believed. We do not need it any more, now that we are fully grown and have a mind and curiosity of our own. However, to release it takes us into the no man's land of "Who am I if I am not that?" Terrifying!

From the word go, that core identity is moulded by all the influences around us, from our first arrival on the planet to finding a place within the family; from the way in which we must adapt to our environment to the way we must interact with people and all our earliest life experiences. But what if that identity no longer serves you and is holding you back? Could you choose another identity? Or better still, can you go back to the 'before' and remember who you truly are, thus ditching this contrived and adapted persona and reclaim your true authentic self?

You can, and the first step is to remember that you are both perfect as your original, innate self, and that you are indeed supremely powerful. You are not fixed or stuck in that adapted overlay of an identity, but because it has got you this far, **the only log that kept you afloat in a dangerous sea**, the alternative, letting go of it, is terrifying. But there is a way. I offer the following vision to help you see why and how you can reclaim your true self and achieve your full glorious potential.

THE GNARLED LOG

Imagine yourself alone on a dark ocean and the only thing keeping you afloat is a gnarled old log, half-submerged, half-rotten, but at least it is holding you up. It is night time, cold and bleak, you are tired and aching for comfort. Suddenly you notice lights in the distance, off to your right. Slowly the lights become clearer until you see they are shining from a great cruise ship. As it moves closer you are able to pick out shapes, until you can start to see everything on board. Now you hear music. The lights are bright, people are dancing and laughing, tables are full of sumptuous food. You want this. As you look down at the rotten old log you are clinging to, you realise it is far from your ideal.

Now the cruise ship travels across your line of vision, you notice good looking crew members in their clean white uniforms. Then they spot you floating in the water and they are beckoning to you to swim over. They are smiling, welcomingly, willing you to make your way towards them. You look down at your rotten old log (your original dysfunctional identity) and then back up at the cruise ship which offers all you've dreamed of (your potential). You are so excited you decide to swim for it. You are inspired and confident, you see your goal and it is enticing enough that you dare to let go of that old log and start to make your way across the water. You are hellbent on getting there and full of confidence that you will make it over that stretch of water, the only obstacle between the old you and all that you wish to be, all that you long for.

As you swim, however, the distance seems longer than you had anticipated, and the ocean more full of swell. You grow increasingly anxious because you are crossing "no man's land" with no obvious support, as you have left your gnarled old log behind. The waves become huge and as it is dark you can only see the cruise ship when you are on the crest of a giant wave, but as you dip down between the waves you feel overwhelmed, terrified, with an increasing sense that you might not make it, that you might drown.

Suddenly, gripped by fear of the unknown (you have let go of your old identity but not yet fully embraced your true one), and what disasters might befall you, you turn around, making your way back to the horrible old gnarled log. You are back where you started and you know this is a huge compromise but you simply didn't have the courage to swim all the way. Now you hang on for dear life to that worn out thing feeling terrible disappointment at the opportunities that you have let pass you by. You are back to square one. You saw a glimpse of what you could be and do, you saw that everything waited for you beyond the fear, all you had ever dreamed of, and you wanted it enough to let go of the past and overcome your fears.

Yet you couldn't quite make it, you lost your nerve partway there, and now you have missed the boat.

On a dark ocean with no landmarks to show us the way we are terrified that we are going to drown. So to let go of that constructed identity that has kept us afloat until now, feels like letting go of life itself. To release that whole dysfunctional persona we must let go of something intimately familiar that saved us when we were very young, when it was our life raft. With it gone, we would find ourselves in a territory where, for a moment, we don't know who we are. To become that blank canvas, we would not know the rules, we would not know how the game is played, we would have no boundaries and no rules, and the thought of this stops us from letting go of our 'gnarled log'. Yet the very things we fear are in fact our true freedom.

The secret is, in order to become the very things you really want and deserve and to be, you have to let go of the past and step into the future (see www.letinto.com). You must be courageous enough to take a leap of faith in order to travel to that magical new landscape of opportunities. Sometimes this is prompted by the 'gnarled log' of our old identity no longer keeping us afloat, at other times it is prompted by the bright and shining light of a new goal beckoning us forward so strongly that we actually make it across the dark night of the soul. By making the crossing, persevering through the fear you will ultimately reach a happier and more fulfilled landscape where you can enjoy all you want while relaxing into finally being your true self. That is why, once you have let go of the old way of being you, it is vital to keep going towards your goal no matter how tricky and at times terrifying, the crossing becomes.

As adults we sense there is more, there are dreams and goals and sometimes we know what they are but often we do not. We want to find them and we strive to reach them. To help us find our way we may seek out a wisdom-keeper, counsellor, coach or therapist who will shine a light on that dark ocean and show us not only the cruise ship of our full potential, but also that it is safe to let go and swim to our dreams. They inspire us and with their wisdom tucked under our belts we find the courage to go for it! But after swimming for a while and no longer bathed in the light of encouragement or support from our mentor, we start to lose momentum and confidence. It is then that our old familiar but dysfunctional persona beckons us back. We forget all we have just learned from our therapist and go back to believing we need that old identity, because are convinced that without it our very survival is at risk. In that moment, basically, we have become once again **the infant who cannot survive without their milk.**

Often, the only thing that motivates us to "swim for it" is when we recognise that old adapted identity has truly become a burden rather than a lifesaver . For example "This isn't what I want, I don't want to be the one who has always got the responsibility on my shoulders, I don't want to be the one who is always having to follow other people's rules" or "I don't want to keep having to be the person who must always remain invisible". In that moment we have recognised that the old persona is not really our true self. Then let go, take the risk of jumping into the unknown, we swim for it "I claim my right to have what I want in my life" which is exactly what we have come to Earth to do.

Remember, getting there takes great courage and determination. It is so frightening to be in that unknown territory because stepping away from the very safeguards you put up, the very way of coping that you developed, means stepping into the abyss and potentially to die, to disappear, to not have YOU any more. The reality is that you are actually stepping INTO the REAL YOU instead of a false you, but the fear of letting go of that false you, places you where no matter how good life is, no matter how well things are going and no matter how strongly you are getting on, you will always ping back as if a piece of elastic attaches you to the old dysfunctional paradigms, to your half-submerged gnarled log.

To slot back into that old original identity YOU manipulate everyone and everything into recreating the old wound. But you don't realise you are doing it. Once you have succeeded in re-clothing yourself in that old, unhappy identity, you feel sorry for yourself saying "There you are, see, I am the one that....gets abandoned, or isn't good enough, or gets betrayed, or loses out, or can't have what they want" etc. You shake your head and say "How did I end up here again? This is the very place I've been trying to get away from and I thought I'd done it, I thought I'd cracked it, I thought I'd sorted it out." The answer is, you are back where you started because you moved all the pieces on your life's chessboard to put yourself there. Why? Not just fear of the unknown, but also because you had to revisit the old painful place in order to learn from it again.

The way forward is to embrace your new persona, but the only way you can do that is to start by going back. Back and back to before you incarnated, before you took on the cloak of any human identity. Back to when you were made of stardust and simply floating in the universe. Back to the core you, the real you, the person who decided that they wanted to come to planet Earth and learn through their own set challenges and adversity. Then ask yourself who is that YOU?

Then quietly instruct yourself to remember the truth of WHO YOU TRULY ARE. Meditate in stillness on this. Allow that warm recognition of balance and perfection to fill you. Once you have re-touched the core of your innate self, then without any fear of being abandoned, betrayed, hurt, basically DYING, hold that feeling in your head and your heart. The knowledge of WHO YOU TRULY ARE, and walk forward to embrace your life exactly as you want it. By being your SELF, expressing YOUR GIFTS as they were originally meant to be expressed, you will be living authentically and without fear. Remember, by listening to and caring for, reassuring and cherishing your own wounded child pieces, you will have fear tamed and mastered. It is then that nothing will stop you, not the wildest, darkest or deepest ocean. You will make it to your full potential.

After reading this you might feel motivated to let go of your old gnarled log, so here to inspire you to keep going till you reach your full potential, is a quote from *Nisargadatta.*

"There can always be moments when one feels empty and estranged. Such moments are most desirable for it means the soul has cast its moorings and is sailing for distant places, it's absolute truth and authenticity.

This is detachment -- when the old is over and the new has not yet come. It is natural to feel some fear, the state of limbo may be distressing, but there is really nothing to be afraid of. Remember this instruction: whatever you come across - go beyond".

CHAPTER 12
Ending at the Beginning

A NEW ERA

There were whispers in the air of a major ending, a catastrophe perhaps, back when the year 2012 approached. Humans had become aware that something momentous was about to happen and many feared the world or humanity would somehow come to a halt. Some headed off into the wilderness to hide and become self-sufficient, away from the impending 'catastrophe' whatever it might be. Others started to search for meaning, so became attached to religions that preached atonement or a great judgement in which only the chosen would be 'saved'. Yet others waited, curious, unsure what it was but feeling deep down inside sensing that something was about to end. And the fears were, as always, caused by lack of knowledge. Those who feared a catastrophe which would mean a grand finale, were dealing in half-truths and completely forgetting that everything is a circle.

As an Astrologer I became fascinated by the Mayan prophecies which had always predicted a major cosmic shift, that something significant would indeed end in 2012. The extraordinarily accurate Mayan calendar was prophesying a significant ending, but as an Astrologer I could see that if it was clearly the end of a cycle, this meant it was also the beginning of the next cycle.

So I travelled to Guatemala to work closely with the Mayan priests, to learn as much as I could of their traditions, their ancestral wisdom and most of all to understand their phenomenally accurate ancient calendar, from which the prophecy about 2012 had come. To see how they had, since ancient times so precisely mapped the movements of the heavenly bodies, and to comprehend their extraordinary interpretations of these movements, was a wonderful revelation. I soon had confirmation that the shift which was about to occur was much more than an ending, it marked a transition from one major cycle of influence to another. They had clearly marked alignments and planetary cycles, and through observing the precession of the equinoxes, the Mayans were able to decipher that Earth went through regular 2,165 year cycles. On a certain date in 2012 we were about to reach the end of one of those cycles and slide into the next one. An epoch where life on Earth and humanity would gradually shift out of the cycle of Pisces and come under the influence of Aquarius.

This meant therefore, that we were about to close a chapter in human learning and open a new one, the Aquarius cycle. Just as people born under the sign of Aquarius share certain characteristics, so this new age would develop to hold the essence of those same characteristics. Leaving behind the Piscean age we humans would leave behind an era of dependency when we had looking outside of ourselves for power and truth, while believing in martyrdom and victimhood. When the priest had authority over our spirituality, the doctor had authority over our bodies and the school moulded our minds. But from 2012 and for the next 2,165 years, humanity would be increasingly embracing the power of the individual and the need to go within for all the answers, mental, physical, emotional and spiritual. The Aquarian age would be an age of seekers, not without but within. This new age is about so many wonderful changes including individuality, fair mindedness, acceptance and balancing of all types with non-judgement, innovation humanitarianism, originality and scientific advancement.

We were all in this boat together, travelling along the time lines, sliding increasingly away from the Piscean era and into the Aquarian age. So it seems that those of us who chose to incarnate at this moment chose to live through a very exciting historical shift in humanity's pattern, from Piscean thinking and behaviour on Earth, to Aquarian. Though March of 2012 was when the equinox point moved out of the constellation Pisces and into the constellation Aquarius, the shift had been gradually approaching this point for many years. Listen with new ears to the lyrics of the famous song written in 1967 for the musical Hair "...this is the dawning of the Age of Aquarius" by Rado and Ragni.

...Harmony and understanding
Sympathy and trust abounding
No more falsehoods or derisions
Golden living dreams of visions
Mystic crystal revelation
And the mind's true liberation...

What a momentous and fascinating time to be experiencing life here on Earth, to be leaving behind an age which embraced the concept of dependency on authority figures, of belief in rescuers and victims, and embracing an age that champions personal responsibility, acceptance of all quirks and kinds of humanity, rebalancing of the sexes (to be straight, gay, bi, or assign yourself a new gender), equalising of humans (icons being torn down or exposed and the poor and needy being increasingly supported), awareness and care for our planet, space exploration accessible to the masses plus the ever increasing advancement in scientific solutions to problems including A.I. Though we are still existing within a decreasing influence left over from the Piscean Age, we are now well and truly in the Aquarian age. It is with fascination that I watch how media reports have ceased to keep humans on pedestals (celebrities, royalty, politicians) but make a point of bringing them down from their high perch to be simply another human like you or I, and how those who have been abused or kept down are now given a voice and justice. Also how the wave of inclusion and acceptance is transitioning rapidly into respect for and fair treatment of those who were condemned for their innate sexuality and preferences, disabilities and setbacks, to tolerance, inclusion and fair treatment for all. We are learning to take personal responsibility and recognise our own power to make the world a better place. The first step is ceasing to judge as we recognise that each time we point the finger of accusation or condemnation, there are three fingers pointing back at ourselves.

The Aquarian age is less sentimental, less dependent, less needy. Each human now stands as an individual, developing and strengthening their OWN inner Light, which grows ever brighter, until they are personally illuminated and strong enough to stand alongside other humans in groups that will make phenomenal advances and improvements for us and our planet, perhaps even our galaxy. Aquarius is associated with space exploration and care for our inner and outer environment, and a more scientific approach to the protection of all that sustains us here on earth.

Impermanence or transformation is an inevitable and definite part of life. The ancient peoples had nature as their guide. They lived with it and in it, in harmony with its energies and seasons. Nature was the library, the teacher, the support and the source of all life. We have travelled far from those times, yet we yearn to reconnect with that ancient knowledge where people were guided and sustained by what was all around them, from the stars in the sky to the animals and plants in their environment. That is why there has been an upsurge in the fascination with and desire to learn Shamanism, a method by which we can go back to the old ways of connecting with and being supported by all in the natural and spirit world. Through Shamanism we can interpret the meanings of animal and plant behaviour and learn to connect, receiving messages and healing from them as the ancients used to. There are so many clues available to us on our Earth walk, we need to re-learn how to listen to and look for them.

The law of attraction says you must vibrate in sympathy with what you wish to manifest. When you are in tune with the natural world and the helpful spirits that inhabit it, your life will unfold with far more ease and far less drama. Then, with an awareness of all the help available to you from your environment, you will joyfully manifest your life.

BACK TO THE BEGINNING. REMEMBER WHO YOU TRULY ARE

I encourage you to use all of the teachings in this book to hold steady and keep going, to swim on, and reach your full potential. To be reborn by remembering who you truly are, a wise being who chose this adventure, and whose core is LOVE. To care for your wounded child pieces while heading forward, so that you can reclaim your power fearlessly and no longer be hampered by the restrictions of the past. And by persevering through the dark ocean of uncertainty, to reach the magical, exciting and brightly lit *cruise ship* of living fearlessly and lovingly in synchronicity with everything and everyone in your sphere. I know you CAN do it!

When you step into trust and gratitude you start to harmonise with the energies of the universe you live in, instead of fighting against or criticising them. By trusting that all is unfolding for the best and exactly as it should, you feel supported and with that gratitude to be alive, you feel love. Consequently you bring joy to every day of your life.

Embrace your uniqueness, you are a shining Light, an original and precious being. Have you ever seen one tree exactly the same as another, or one sparkling crystal identical to another? There is no-one like you. You are that rare and sacred gift of light and shadow. Remember who you truly are and embrace your own beauty and your perfection, take the brakes (of fear) off and make the most of this opportunity to be on Earth.

If the words "ending" and "beginning" were only invented by humans on their Earth walk to make sense of their world and that in reality endings and beginnings did not exist, then there is never a void and as everything is a circle, each apparent ending will merely be the next beginning.

So, WHY ON EARTH are you here now? Your sole purpose is Soul learning. To let go of judgement and TO BECOME COMPLETELY AND UNCONDITIONALLY LOVING

Always remember, YOU are the power, enjoy the ride!

Lightning Source UK Ltd.
Milton Keynes UK
UKHW010723181219
355598UK00001B/28/P